WHILE TIME REMAINS

A North Korean Defector's Search for Freedom in America

YEONMI PARK

THRESHOLD EDITIONS

New York   London   Toronto   Sydney   New Delhi

Threshold Editions
An Imprint of Simon & Schuster, Inc.
1230 Avenue of the Americas
New York, NY 10020

First Threshold Editions hardcover edition February 2023

THRESHOLD EDITIONS and colophon are trademarks of Simon & Schuster, Inc.

For information about special discounts for bulk purchases, please contact Simon & Schuster Special Sales at 1-866-506-1949 or business@simonandschuster.com.

The Simon & Schuster Speakers Bureau can bring authors to your live event. For more information or to book an event, contact the Simon & Schuster Speakers Bureau at 1-866-248-3049 or visit our website at www.simonspeakers.com.

Interior design by Esther Paradelo

Manufactured in the United States of America

10   9   8   7   6   5   4   3   2   1

Library of Congress Cataloging-in-Publication Data has been applied for.

ISBN 978-1-6680-0331-2
ISBN 978-1-6680-0333-6 (ebook)

Contents

Yeonmi-ya,
tigers leave behind a coat,
and men leave behind a name;
make yours good and lasting.

—MY FATHER

Foreword

If the hypothetical moralism of the Left had any grounding in reality, it would be hard to imagine anyone who those of that political stripe would celebrate more than Ms. Yeonmi Park, who escaped with little more than her skin and bones from the tender mercies of the brutal North Korean regime. She has everything the heroic victim (hypothetically) requires: all the "intersectional" virtues. She is an immigrant, and female; someone who had been subject to truly dreadful abuse from someone truly tyrannical (and from the government agents at his family's diabolical disposal); she was genuinely starved; she was enslaved—along with her mother, literally bought and sold—and exploited sexually, at a very young age.

Her "education" as a young girl consisted of little more than the propagandistic glorification of her persecutors; subjugation to the lies they told (and constantly) about everyone else everywhere in the world—including the explicit demonization of Americans, blamed continually for the utter catastrophic failure that North Korea clearly and irrefutably constitutes. Park emerged from all that, and worse, to become a voice of freedom; to become someone who not only talked about speaking truth to power but actually did so; to become, despite her relative and starvation-induced frailty, a true thorn in the side of one of the worst dictatorships the world has ever managed to produce.

In that respect, she is reminiscent of Ayaan Hirsi Ali, another woman whom I thought in my initial ignorance, years ago, would be a positive darling of every feminist worth her salt in the West. Ayaan Hirsi Ali: another woman, another immigrant, a victim of female genital mutilation; someone whom, with extraordinary bravery, dared to face down the authoritarian religious hypocrites who wished to doom her to a life of unquestioning subordination and obedience. Her reward? She was, not least, identified as an "anti-Muslim extremist" by the *Field Guide* to such individuals published by the Southern Poverty Law Center, an appallingly self-righteous and utterly hypocritical leftist organization—a group of lawyers purporting to serve as a "catalyst for racial justice in the South and beyond, working in partnership with communities to dismantle white supremacy, strengthen intersectional movements, and advance the human rights of all people," and employing all the reprehensible clanging idiot-jargon of the radical narcissists of compassion to do so. However, because Ali had the gall not to toe the party line and trumpet the evils of the capitalist West (quite the contrary: she regards the West as exceptionally admirable, particularly in comparative terms), she is persona non grata on the Left.

There is no one more annoying to the ideological activists of the radical Left than a minority woman who doesn't know her proper political place; no one more irritating than someone whom, according to the dictates of that God-forsaken jargon-ridden conceptual scheme, has "internalized their oppression," and who therefore stands up for the hypothetical enemy, which must always and invariably be, by the standards of the pseudo-illuminated puritans in question, the West, the West, the West.

Thus, Ms. Park has been subject to treatment very similar to that which befell Ali, although arguably even more extensively. She employed her YouTube channel to draw attention to the plight of the North Koreans, particularly the women who experienced the same horrors that befell her and her mother. She pointed out, with all due accuracy, the utter complicity of the damned Chinese Communist Party in supporting that appalling, tyrannical regime—allowing the continued slave-trading of North Korean women in China, and using the cruel, genocidal, and megalomaniac Kim dynasty as a convenient and nuclear-armed goad to prod and threaten the West. And that regime poses no mean threat: North Korea's military is the fourth largest in the world and is nuclear armed. Furthermore, as Ms. Park points out, the anti-American rhetoric employed by the Kim family's nest of devils is ultimately inflammatory, in the most atomic of manners: North Korean schoolchildren are taught that the total destruction of American cities by the very weapons just described is something not only fully justified but to be devoutly desired. YouTube's response? The demonetization of Yeonmi's channel—not once, but repeatedly, with no explanation. Remember "Don't be evil"? The much-paraded motto of the very Google that now owns YouTube? Remember when that motto was scrapped? Every wonder why? Look no further than the pathetic kowtowing to the Chinese overlords that characterizes such behavior and derive your own conclusions.

If the Cinderella story had been written by someone much grimmer than the Brothers Grimm, the star could well be the author of the current book. After escaping from the utter prison of North Korea; after surviving the sex slavery imposed on her (and her mother, simultaneously) in China; after educating herself in an absolutely unlikely manner in South Korea, she made her way to the United States, and enrolled in Columbia University, a once-great beacon of Western freedom. To say that this was the dream of a lifetime is to radically overstate the case; this was something undreamed of, something outside the realm of all reasonable possibility. Ms. Park, guided by the spirit of her entrepreneurial father, truly valued education—had endeavoured in all ways to educate herself as thoroughly as possible, in the traditional sense, when she managed to make her way to South Korea, where she pored over, among other works, the books of the great George Orwell, author of *Animal Farm* and *1984*.

And what happened when she entered the hallowed halls of that august institution of higher education?

She encountered the same ideology that had corrupted her homeland and doomed its inhabitants to a life in hell. Of course, it was America: it was Totalitarianism Lite, offered, as all such things are in this over-coddled and narcissistic time, as a convenient fashion statement; a faux identity; a means of parading unearned moral virtue while biding time as an oppressor-in-training—the inevitable and truly desired fate of every virtue-signaling Ivy League graduate. She was upbraided by her pathetic professors for daring to admire Jane Austen, whose books "promote female oppression, racism, colonialism, and white supremacy" and "propagate the idea that women are inferior to men; that only white males are fully evolved and capable of higher-level thinking; that salvation is only achievable through the dogma of Christianity" (of course; or else). And Yeonmi learned that she better think and feel that way—even when listening to "Western" classical music (or else). There was nothing more unacceptable at Columbia than to be a "SIX HIRB": a sexist, intolerant, xenophobic, homophobic, Islamophobic, racist bigot.

Yeonmi Park grew up in a totalitarian nightmare. As a child, she roasted and consumed insects to survive, when she could find them. As someone from a poor family (and that genuinely meant poor in North Korea) she had to bring five rabbit pelts to class and hand them over to maintain any social standing whatsoever with the propagandists who passed as teachers. She grew up among people whose dying wish was meat stew and rice. She was subject to the worst dictatorship on the planet—maybe the worst dictatorship ever promulgated, although the competition for that vaunted position is very fierce. She came to the US, miraculously, and encountered fools dallying with the same ideas that had made her life something almost unbelievably harsh—certainly that, by Western standards. She attempted with all her heart, as she is doing in the present volume, to warn us here in our luxury and comfort not to fall prey to the same ideological temptations that doomed the Soviet Union and all its satellites and that still possess the billion-plus people in China, much to the detriment of that country's beleaguered citizens and the rest of the world. Who led the rush to lockdown? China. Who copied the actions of that terrible state?

The cowardly fools of the West.

Park is warning us not to continue to do so.

Will we listen?

Perhaps.

Perhaps not.

—JORDAN B. PETERSON

Preface

O n October 4, 1993, I was born in darkness.

For the previous half-century, the North Korean regime could only sustain the illusion of socialist "self-sufficiency" with charitable aid from the Soviet Union. When the USSR dissolved in 1991, the aid dried up. Money, goods, and energy imports to North Korea collapsed. Then came the floods. The country's arable lands, inadequate to feed its 21 million people even in the best of times, were flooded. The coal mines that powered the country's meager electricity supply were flooded, too. By the autumn of 1993, in the house where I was born, the darkness had already arrived. The famine was coming.

Juche is the official religion and political ideology of the North Korean state, and it means that North Korea is self-sufficient because it is ruled by a single leader. In reality, it is one of the least self-sufficient countries on Earth. It could not exist without help from Moscow during the Cold War, just as it cannot exist without help from Beijing today. With no actual experience of producing or distributing enough food to feed its population, it was all but inevitable that the regime would preside over a catastrophic famine. It had no idea how to respond.

The government in Pyongyang couldn't come up with a rationing procedure that had any basis in reality. The "eat two meals a day" campaign, in which two meals a day would supposedly be allocated to individual North Koreans in the order determined by their loyalty to the regime, was only meant to convey the illusion that North Koreans in ordinary times were used to three meals. To prepare the country, the government with no plan to feed its people banned the words *famine* and *hunger*, officially terming the struggle to come "The Arduous March."

By the time I was five years old, up to 3.5 million North Koreans had died of starvation. No one knows the real number—it is likely that no one will ever know—because no one kept track.

I was born in Ryanggang Province, in Hyesan, on the Yalu River, which separates North Korea from China. Even if it were run by the Swiss or the Japanese, Hyesan would still be mountainous, dry, and freezing cold. Under the remit of the Kim family, it is a wasteland.

Darkness in Hyesan is total. It is not just the absence of light, power, and food. It is the absence of dignity, sanctuary, and hope.

Darkness in Hyesan is hunting for cockroaches and dragonflies to eat on the way to school so you won't get distracted by hunger in class, where the teacher leads you in songs with titles like "Nothing to Envy." It is witnessing public executions on your way back home. It is watching your parents and neighbors hauled away by police for the crime of collecting insects and plants for their children to eat. It is watching the authorities take away the little that does grow on collective farms for the "Glory of the State." It is eternal night.

On the night of March 30, 2007, when I was thirteen years old, I escaped North Korea into China. I didn't escape in search of freedom, or liberty, or safety. I escaped in search of a bowl of rice.

EVER SINCE, I have always said that being born in North Korea is the best thing that ever happened to me. It is of course, in a literal sense, the very *worst* thing that could happen to anyone. But now, looking back on it from a distance of nearly half my life, from my apartment in Chicago, that part of my life gave me an appreciation for simple human existence that I'm not sure I would have gotten elsewhere.

It is not just the basic provisions of everyday life—nutritious food, clean water, light, heat, a bed to sleep in—that I now regard as minor miracles. I feel a deep appreciation and awe for human freedom as a whole: the right to exist, the ability to think, to love, to walk or sit without looking over my shoulder, to take two consecutive breaths uninterrupted by fear. I feel that I have an unusual capacity for gratitude now, and I owe it to the sixteen-year nightmare that was my previous life. In the most twisted way imaginable, I actually regard that time as a blessing.

I say sixteen years because for the first two years after my mother and I crossed the frozen Yalu River into China, our nightmare was prolonged. We found our bowl of rice, but nearly at the price of our lives. As I recounted in my first book, *In Order to Live*, for those twenty-three months in China—before we traveled through the Gobi Desert to eventual safety in South Korea—we were slaves. The people who helped us cross the river from North Korea were human traffickers, and once they had us in China, they traded and sold us like commodities. In those years, we were made to serve as the personal bodily property of Chinese farmers who viewed North Korean women as inhuman vessels for sex and violence. They fed us rice, but for reasons that were no more virtuous or compassionate than the reason North Korean prisons feed inmates gruel.

It was in China that I learned how the North Korean regime was able to weather the famine and continue subjecting millions of people, up through the present day, to what the United Nations has described as "a modern-day holocaust." The same regime that surveils 1.4 billion Chinese people, which controls almost every aspect of their lives, and which has made real progress toward wiping out the Tibetan and Uyghur peoples, keeps the Kim family in control of Pyongyang. The Chinese Communist Party has long since replaced the USSR as the chief enabler of the modern-day holocaust. While I was in China, not knowing any better, I started to believe that the whole world must be nothing more than variations on a North Korean theme: fear, cold, abuse, despair.

There was only one time in my life when I ever came close to not having the strength to see it through—and it was after I had already left North Korea. It was in China.

BY 2009, I got my first taste of freedom in South Korea. There I met Christian missionaries who worked all over the world, and in 2013, they invited me on a trip to places I'd hardly ever heard of: Tyler, Texas and Atlanta, Georgia. Eager to travel, I accepted their invitation. I was nineteen years old, and went to America.

And I was saved.

There are a number of places that are even more spectacular in person than they are in legend. The Great Pyramid of Giza. The Taj Mahal. The Sistine Chapel. The same is rarely true of countries as a whole. Most societies have founding myths—national origin stories—that serve certain internal political purposes, or project some desired image to the outside world. But these myths don't always reflect reality, at least to outsiders. France's commitment to *fraternité*, for example, isn't immediately obvious to visitors to Paris.

The United States remains the only country that, for me, was even more magnificent in person than its reputation. It wasn't just the friendliness of the people, who exude the confidence and openness of men and women living, worshiping, and loving as they please. It was the sense of *excitement*, of dynamism, a certain electricity in the air and in personal interactions. These were clearly the descendants, I thought, of those who overturned imperialism and slavery, defeated fascism and communism, invented motion pictures and jazz, eliminated diseases, created the internet, and landed on the moon. I knew then that I wanted to live with them, to call them my friends and family—even, if I could, to be one of them.

In January of 2022, I did. I became an American citizen. I sometimes have to pinch myself as a reminder that it's true. I never imagined that I would have the degree of freedom and personal liberty that I've been able to enjoy in the United States. The simple fact that I wrote this book using nothing but my own memories, my own conscience, and my own perspective—unencumbered by censorship or threats of legal repercussions—is a testament to the miracle of American life.

THE IMPETUS for this book came from something that happened to me in Chicago in the summer of 2020, when I was assaulted and robbed in broad daylight in front of my young child. The bystanders who watched it happen refused to intervene because of the color of my skin, and that of the assailants. I go into detail about this incident in chapter 7. But in that seminal experience, I realized two things that made me want to write the pages you now hold in your hand: first, that many of my fellow Americans have lost the ability to appreciate the glory of this country the way I do, and second, that many of them are not able to recognize certain threats the way I can.

When I tell my American friends and colleagues that certain developments in the United States remind me of North Korea, they typically cock their heads and smirk. When I clarify that I'm referring not to the quality of life or system of government, of course, but to the control of institutions by a small class of people eager to punish dissenters, it doesn't help—they still look away in embarrassment. People who have no problem believing that I was able to escape and recover from thirteen years of brainwashing by the Dear Leader also seem to think I've fallen prey in a few short years to indoctrination from the "far right." And that's exactly my point.

"Right wing" is one of those terms of abuse I understood only after a number of my fellow Americans used it in a concerted and sometimes successful attempt to harass and censor me. In this context at least, I've learned that it does not refer to a set of social and economic preferences on the spectrum of American political possibilities. It means "disloyal"—disloyal to the tastes, opinions, values, and preferences of the financial, political, and cultural elite. The disloyalty of the lower and working classes to the ruling class.

If those circumstances remind me of aspects of North Korea, where I grew up and you (most likely) did not, does that make me "far right"?

I have no idea, to be honest, because "right" and "left" are categories that haven't helped me understand much about my new home. I understand these mostly as outdated terms that stopped having any explanatory power sometime before I arrived in America in 2013, and that survive only as tools of social organization wielded by oligarchs, elites, and political operatives to police the boundaries of acceptable thought. All of which is to say that I have no ideological commitment to the success or failure of Democrats or Republicans, to liberals or conservatives, or to the left wing or right wing, insofar as they exist in any meaningful way.

What I am committed to is an absolutist ideology of individual rights and freedom, of the kind that Thomas Jefferson and Martin Luther King Jr. shared in common. I'm also committed to resisting any encroachments on it, which is why I draw on my knowledge and experience of North Korea to illuminate—not exaggerate—threats to liberty in America. And I do see threats on the horizon.

That's why I wrote this book. Because I escaped hell on earth and walked across the desert in search of freedom, and found it. Because I made it to the promised land, and had a son, whose first breath was as an American citizen. Because I don't want anything bad to ever happen to my new home. Because I want us—I need us—to keep the darkness at bay.

Because I need your help to save our country, while time remains.

American Bastards

The classroom is cold and decrepit. It smells of the spent wood disintegrating into white ash in the furnace in a corner of the room. The wall above the furnace is stained black, and as the wood crumbles under its own weight the embers crack and pop. I'm all but indistinguishable from my two dozen classmates, all of us dressed in identical, run-down winter uniforms, sitting on the concrete floor, crammed together for warmth. Some of us are hungry, others are starving. A few struggle to stay awake; their eyes roll back and their heads fall as they nod off.

Better to sleep than to be awake and hungry, I think.

I'm stuck on the far side of the back row—the one farthest from the furnace—with other "struggling" kids. *Why can't I be a better student,* I ask myself, *and get to sit in the front?* I close my eyes and clench my fists, wishing for it to come true so the teacher will move me up front, closer to the heat. I open my eyes and there I am, still in the back. I know why, of course: I'm bad at studying. I often have no idea what my teacher and classmates are talking about. History is impossible to memorize, math is like a foreign language.

The only way to make up for being a poor student is to exceed the "rabbit pelt quota"—each student must deliver five furs per semester, ostensibly for the army's winter uniforms but in reality for the school administrators to sell—and to answer questions about our "Socialist Paradise" with a fervent, almost hysterical passion. I'm not good at doing these, either.

"Park Yeonmi!" The teacher's harsh tone wakes me up from my stupor.

"Yes, Teacher?" I answer. A shiver runs down my spine.

"Recite the full title of our Great Leader!"

I stall, trying to buy time to gather my thoughts before opening my mouth. If the wrong answer comes out, there could be consequences for my family.

"Quick! We don't have all day."

"Our great comrade Kim Jong Il," I venture, "the general secretary of the Workers' Party of Korea, the chairman of the DPRK National Defense Commission, and the supreme commander of the Korean People's Army . . ." I mumble the last few words, in case they're not exactly right.

"Very good!" the teacher responds.

I breathe a sigh of relief. My family will be okay today. But then . . .

"Now sing the national anthem!" the teacher yells.

Oh no. How does it start, again? I can't remember. I panic. "Umm . . ."

"Park Yeonmi! Sing the national anthem!"

Why is everyone staring at me? Why isn't anyone helping me? I wish my sister Eunmi were here. I want my *umma*. I feel a lump in my throat and a tear run down my cheek, and wipe it away with the back of my hand as quickly as possible.

"What is this? Are you even stupider than I thought, girl? Sing the national anthem—*now*!"

I have no choice. I shut my eyes and open my mouth, praying for the right melody to emerge. Miraculously, it works! The words come out—I'm singing! Right? Or . . . what is that sound? It's tinny, like a bad recording being played through a loudspeaker, and at a deafening volume. Is it coming from outside? It's not. It's coming from me. Oh no . . .

"O'er the ramparts we watched, were so gallantly streaming?"

I'm singing, but the voice isn't mine. It's the recording from my naturalization course, the line in the national anthem that gives me so much trouble.

"O'er"? Ramparts? And why is there a question mark?

More importantly, *can anyone else hear this?* How on earth is it coming from inside of me?

"What is this nonsense?" the teacher yells.

My stomach freezes. They all can hear it. I'm gripped by terror.

"Stop it and sing the anthem of our beloved motherland!"

"And the rocket's red glare," I go on, not able to shut my mouth. "The bombs bursting in air."

"GUARDS!" the teacher shrieks. "GUARDS!"

I go quiet, close my lips, and open my eyes. The room is pitch black now, but I still smell the burning wood. The teacher and my classmates are gone, but I hear whispers, feet shuffling on the concrete floor. There must be someone there. I look to the only source of light, the embers in the furnace. They disappear and reappear like flashing lights. Someone is pacing back and forth in front of the furnace.

I hear a loud, artillery-like whistling noise. I look outside the window, and it's only a flare. It lights up the night sky, throwing a crash of white light into the classroom. I turn around to look at the furnace again.

Two soldiers advance toward me with fixed bayonets, obscuring the man behind them. He's in a black suit, pacing back and forth in front of the furnace, and throws a lit cigar onto the floor.

I wake up screaming.

I sit up in bed, my palms pressed down on damp sheets, my back straight as a board. I'm in my apartment in Morningside Heights, in New York City. I see now that I'm safe, that it was just a dream. But it takes several minutes for my muscles to relax, my insides to resettle. It's almost 4 a.m. There's hardly any noise coming from the street below. My skin is still sweaty, but I turn the heat up a little anyway, and a lamp on.

MY GREATEST wish came true in 2015 when I immigrated to the United States of America. Never in my wildest dreams could I have imagined such an ending to my escape from North Korea. I had previously traveled there in 2013 as part of a volunteer mission program based in Tyler, Texas, southeast of Dallas. I had no money then and didn't speak much English, but I'd found America to be a vast and stunningly beautiful country, and Americans far from what I'd learned growing up.

It is customary in North Korean schools to use anti-American propaganda even to teach math. "There were five American tanks and the North Korean Army destroyed four of them. How many are left?" That kind of thing. And of course we could never just use the word *American* unadorned by any insults, which would have been seen as suspiciously respectful. It was always "American bastards," "Yankee devils," or "big-nosed Yankees."

We were also taught in school that, unlike the great people of North Korea, American bastards were not human. I don't mean that Americans are "dehumanized" in North Korean schools—I mean we were taught, quite literally, that Americans are cold-blooded reptiles with horns and pitchfork tails. This nonsensical myth remains so persistent throughout the lives of poor, uneducated North Koreans that my own mother was stunned when she met the lovely American co-author of my previous book, Maryanne Vollers, in person. "Yeonmi-ya," my mother said to me after Maryanne shook her hand and gave her a hug. "This American lady feels warm." "Yes, Umma!" I replied. "She is a human like us." She was quite shocked.

Schools in North Korea also used graphic imagery to accompany the official state narrative about the United States. Our textbooks and even some classroom walls were covered in grotesque renderings of blond-haired, green-eyed American soldiers with massive noses murdering Korean civilians, or else *being* killed by brave North Korean students wielding pitchforks and bayonets. On many mornings, we would line up in the freezing cold during recess and take turns stabbing dummies of American GIs with sticks whittled into spears, in order to keep ourselves sharp for when the enemy would inevitably return.

The message was clear: The threat from America is real, it is imminent, and you are all in immediate danger.

I remember being so scared at night that Yankee devils would bomb and invade Hyesan, kill my parents, and torture me and Eunmi for pleasure.

Of course, the propaganda taught in North Korean schools is not limited to lies about America. We were also taught that the Kim family has supernatural powers and that their very existence is a gift from

Heaven to the North Korean people. Kim Il Sung (1912–1994), the founder of North Korea, was revered not just as a god-*like* figure, but as an actual deity. He was so successful at developing this cult of personality that even when he died of a heart attack, no one questioned the fact of his supposed immortality.

The birthday of his son, Kim Jong Il (1941–2011), is known as *Kwang Myong Song-jol*, "Day of the Shining Star." According to legend, the night he was born, a bright star appeared in the sky above Paektu Mountain—the highest point in North Korea—and guerrilla fighters carved messages on trees proclaiming, "Oh! Korea! The Paektu Star Was Born!" and "Three Heroes Shining in Korea with the Spirit of Mount Paekdu: Kim Il Sung, Kim Jong-suk [his first wife], and *Kwang Myong Song*." More than one observer has noted the similarity between the "morning star" of Jesus Christ in the Book of Revelation and the "shining star" of Kim Jong Il, son of North Korea's founding god.

Like all totalitarian heirs of Joseph Stalin, the Kim regime knows that it is important to control people's bodies, but more important to control their thoughts. In 1934, the German novelist Heinrich Mann referred to the power of the Nazi state as the "dictatorship of the mind," "complete control over the whole intellectual and spiritual life of the nation." Jang Jin-sung, a former North Korean poet and propaganda official who eventually defected to South Korea, called the mass enslavement of a population's mental life as "emotional dictatorship."

Like aspects of Muammar Gaddafi's Libya and revolutionary Iran, the Kim regime controls the flow of information in North Korea the way drug lords control the flow of narcotics: systematically eliminating sources of competition, centralizing production, and determining distribution.

———

MY FATHER, Park Jin Sik, was an entrepreneur from Hyesan, and he dedicated his life to doing what little he could to improve the lives of his family. Dissatisfied with the paltry living he eked out working at a defunct factory, he decided to work for himself instead in the black market: first selling cigarettes in the surrounding townships, and eventually smuggling copper and other metals into neighboring China. Such business was risky, but the profits were worth it. My father was a natural salesman and knew how to evade the authorities and do well by his customers. By the time I was seven years old, we were living happy, relatively prosperous lives.

But when I was nine, the authorities caught my father and sentenced him to hard labor in a camp near Pyongyang, about 550 miles southwest of Hyesan. Umma, my mother, Keum Sook Byeon, was considered to be his accomplice, and was also sentenced to time in prison. During this time, she was regularly interrogated and sexually assaulted. She was eventually sentenced to hard labor for several months for moving her residence from Hyesan to Kowon without the permission of the authorities. For nearly two years, she was "disappeared" for up to forty days at a time.

During that time, I was left alone in Hyesan and my mother's hometown of Kowon with my sister Eunmi, who was thirteen. Up to that point, it was the hardest period of my life.

Eunmi and I had very little food or money, and had to learn harsh lessons in real *Juche*—learning how to catch grasshoppers and dragonflies and roasting them for dinner. When these "protein delicacies" were scarce, we gathered plants from the surrounding hills, if for no other reason than to have something to chew on. I remember crying so hard on certain nights that my eyes went completely dry, even as I continued to convulse and rock back and forth. Worrying I would never see my parents again—that the four of us would never be made whole again—I eventually went numb, feeling a near-total indifference to life. I hadn't yet reached my tenth birthday.

When you hear stories about the apathy and cruelty that ordinary people find themselves resorting to in socialist systems, don't judge them: A human being alienated from her family and facing starvation has been robbed of her capacity to connect with the world around her.

My mother was eventually released from prison early (she was able to bribe a guard), and in 2006, my father was also released after three years in the camp (he had also bribed his prison guards to allow him safe passage to Hyesan with the promise of sending them money upon his return). We were all, at last, reunited. But the initial euphoria of seeing my father again was tempered by the realization that he was not the same person anymore. His joie de vivre was gone, the lines of his mouth sloping downward, his eyes without the spark that had always lit up his face when he told us stories about his adventures doing "business" across North Korea, and even about how he'd heard that other countries were "advancing." (I didn't know what this meant, as I'd never seen a map before.) My father was sick and broken. The four of us were together again in Hyesan, but we were a different family now. The hope that one day we'd be made whole again was lost forever.

It might be difficult for outsiders to grasp, but the life of an ex-offender is exponentially worse than that of an "average" North Korean. There are no reintegration programs, no case managers, no social workers, no employment assistance or opportunities for reentry like in America or Europe. The North Korean ex-con is a pariah, and his family is guilty by association. They are downgraded to the lowest caste and shunned. Their blood is tainted, and all doors to opportunity are closed: No collective farm, factory, military branch, or civil service will take them back.

The possibility of redemption is at the center of all great religions and societies. In North Korea, as in all communist dictatorships, it is inconceivable.

Then, one night, Eunmi disappeared. When she was several hours late returning home, my parents panicked, and they searched for her all over town. The longer the night went on, though, the more it became apparent that Eunmi was not simply missing or hard to find; she was no longer in Hyesan. Eventually, we found a note from her hidden under my pillow: Eunmi had decided she couldn't tolerate our destitution any longer, and escaped across the Yalu River into China. The note instructed me to make contact with a woman on the outskirts of town who was helping her; she would know how to make contact with Eunmi. Her decision was extremely risky, both to her own life and to ours, and caused a lot of anger and fear within our family.

To make matters worse, just before Eunmi's escape, I'd suddenly fallen ill with horrendous abdominal pain and had to be taken to the hospital. I was misdiagnosed with appendicitis and underwent surgery with substandard anesthesia. I woke up mid-procedure and passed out from the pain.

When I regained consciousness in the run-down hospital bed, a few days had passed. Eunmi was gone, and my parents seemed to be on the brink of insanity.

We had no other choice: We needed to make contact with Eunmi. I begged the doctors to remove my stitches, and they reluctantly agreed. Eunmi's handwritten note had given instructions for finding the woman on the outskirts of Hyesan. When we found her, she told us what she'd apparently told Eunmi: In China we would not only find food but also be able to make immediate contact with my sister. At the time, we had no idea how big China was, or what the Chinese government's policy was toward North Korean defectors.

Unbeknownst to my sister, my mother, and me, however, we had all walked into the hands of human traffickers. The woman on the outskirts of Hyesan was in the business of luring North Korean women with the prospects of food and work in China. We were faced with an impossible choice: My mother and I could leave immediately and have a chance to find Eunmi, or lose that opportunity forever and go back home, where there was no food to eat and no possibility of my parents finding employment. I convinced my mother that we had to take that chance.

EVEN THE most hardened critics of the Chinese state express shock and dismay when I explain that, in certain ways, our nightmare began only *after* we left North Korea. In Changbai County, in China's southern Jilin Province, my mother and I were passed from one human trafficker to the next, each time at an increased price. We were eventually sold as "wives" to rural Chinese men who could not find a Chinese wife. (The CCP's one-child policy, brutally implemented in 1980 to slow population growth, resulted in a massive gender imbalance—a generation of "missing women"—due to the preference of many Chinese families for sons rather than daughters.) I was thirteen years old, and my mother was forty-one.

There was no choice for us in the matter. Failure to comply with the men who purchased us would result in our transfer to the Chinese authorities, who would return us to North Korea—where we would have been tortured to death. My mother was sold as a slave-wife to a farmer, while I was purchased as a mistress by a human trafficker. Before we were separated, the man who sold us threatened to rape me. To protect me, my mother offered herself instead. It happened several times, sometimes within earshot and eyesight of me.

The man who kept me as his child-mistress eventually promised to help buy back my mother and even bring my father to China. He stayed true to his word. It was the kind of small mercy I prayed for, but by the time he made good on his promise, I was a different person. What innocence and sanity I'd felt I had left were gone. Eunmi, too, was still missing.

Three months later, my mother and I were reunited. My father's arrival in China three months after that was bittersweet. It coincided with my fourteenth birthday—the best present I could have ever asked for—but by then he was too sick to function. At the time, we didn't know what was wrong with him, but we later discovered that he had colon cancer—it had gone undiagnosed for years while he was in prison. When he underwent a kind of experimental surgery in China, the doctors determined that there was nothing that could be done; cancer had spread throughout most of his body.

In early 2008, my father passed away. At the moment he died, I was tending to him, and I held his motionless body in my arms. It was 7:30 a.m., I remember I'd spent the night before holding him and cutting his fingernails. I was shattered and angry, and felt an indescribable loneliness, even with my mother next to me. The only thing that kept the ultimate darkness at bay was the knowledge that my father, who had been able to find joy, adventure, and love even in a life marked by untold suffering, was suffering no more. Unlike the living, he was at peace.

My mother and I moved my father's body in the dark, with the help of two henchmen hired by the man who called me his mistress. It had to be done under cover of night to avoid detection by Chinese police (my "husband" was only allowed to smuggle in North Korean women, not men). My father was unceremoniously cremated, and to avoid drawing attention, I took his ashes to the top of a hill in Yang-shanzhen, overlooking a river. I buried his remains quickly, afraid that if I said a word in prayer, I would start to cry, and be heard by the police, who would send me back to North Korea.

After a year, the trafficker who had taken me as his mistress fell prey to a desperate gambling addiction. When he could no longer afford to pay for much, he allowed me and my mother to find refuge elsewhere. We were eventually introduced to a group of Christian missionaries who aided North Korean defectors in China by first converting them and then sending them to South Korea.

The path the missionaries used for defectors was arduous and involved crossing the Gobi Desert to Mongolia in the dead of night. My mother and I were part of a small group of eight, including a couple with a toddler. We were cold and hungry and had only the stars and a compass to guide us. After treading the path described by our guides, we were finally discovered by Mongolian border patrol. We were transferred to a military base and processed to be sent to South Korea.

Ever since, I've thought of the Gobi Desert as my deliverance, my personal Red Sea. I remember the feeling of looking up at the sky on the night we spent trekking across the desert: a dumbstruck awe, accompanied by an intense loneliness and feeling of utter insignificance. I recall thinking that if I died that night, of frostbite, or an affliction, or by falling prey to a wild animal, that ultimately, once my mother was gone, no one would ever know or care.

My father used to tell me, "Yeonmi-ya, tigers leave behind a coat, and men leave behind a name; make yours good and lasting." If I died in the desert that night, I would have left behind nothing. My life, I felt, would have been for naught.

Looking up at the tapestry of stars, keeping my legs moving so as not to freeze, trying to help the young couple in our group keep their baby warm, I remember looking back on all that my family and I had endured up to that point—how all of it would have been meaningless unless I could find a way to give it meaning. I promised myself that night that if I made it to the other side—if I survived—I would have to find a way to give it all meaning: to Eunmi's disappearance, to my mother's abuse, to my father's imprisonment and death.

I had to live in order to tell my story, and the story of the 21 million North Koreans still trapped in the darkest place on earth.

My mother and I were lucky to make it to South Korea in one piece. The missionaries who helped us had told us repeatedly to prepare for the possibility of being caught by Chinese authorities and sent back to North Korea. Our only preparation for this eventuality had been the means for a swift departure from our bodies: We'd packed razors and poison.

Nothing brings us into closer touch with the reality of our own biology than when we're stripped of everything that makes us human, and are left with a single attribute: the instinct to survive. As biologists from Charles Darwin to Richard Dawkins have explained, this is what links us so closely with the animal kingdom. But human beings experience an added psychological burden: We must come to terms in advance of death with losing our loved ones, and with our own demise.

I remember preparing myself for suicide. My mother and I had a plan for if we were caught: She had hidden dozens of razor blades in my jacket and a plastic bag full of sleeping pills in her bra. We cried as we rehearsed the steps if we got caught by the authorities. We tried to lighten the emotional burden by reassuring each other that we were lucky to be in such a position at all: to finally escape to freedom, or else to finally be released from hell. Our journey to the other side—wherever that might be—would be together.

It would be to freedom.

THE EXPERIENCE of the previous several months had put me in an almost permanent state of unreality, of questioning whether I was actually experiencing the life I was leading or was merely hallucinating. But when I arrived in Seoul by plane from Mongolia on April 20, 2009, I truly felt like I'd entered a dream.

People in South Korea spoke like us, sort of. I heard strange and unfamiliar words and accents. Time in North Korea is stunted in the 1940s, and thus so was the language people used to communicate and the culture they used as a common framework. Entering South Korea was like traveling through space and time. There were high-speed trains, internet, and people wearing jeans—just like we'd seen in pirated DVDs of South Korean dramas.

I was never a great student, nor did I apply myself to anything intellectual while I lived in North Korea. This all changed when I was given the opportunity in South Korea to obtain a GED for both middle and high school, concurrently.

With the abuse and violence that my mother had suffered at the forefront of my mind, I decided to commit myself to the study of criminal justice. It was an arduous process, thanks not only to the fact that my own educational level was far behind my age, but to the extreme competition for which the South Korean education system is famous. It is consistently ranked at or near the top of education systems world-wide, with some of the highest global marks for pre-college student achievement. I found South Korean kids to be obsessed with educa-tion, eager to pack their free time with tutoring and supplemental courses to get ahead of their classmates—which I could keep up with only by spending every waking hour I had alone, studying and reading as many books as I could. This system has produced a highly skilled workforce and one of the world's top ten economies by nominal GDP, despite the country's having almost no natural resources, a population smaller than Kenya's, and having been one of the poorest areas in the world within living memory.

The education system of South Korea, however, is not particu-larly welcoming to foreigners. For starters, with rare exceptions, all classes are conducted in Korean—a difficult language with many cul-tural nuances and written in a unique alphabet known as *Hangul*. Interestingly, many subjects like law and medicine require Korean students to learn English, but not for purposes of communication—it's to allow them to absorb information from English textbooks and the internet.

Beyond the cultural and linguistic differences, foreign students in South Korean schools have also reported difficulty keeping up with the sheer volume of material. As a native North Korean—and very much considered a foreigner by my countrymen to the south—I struggled to keep up.

Due to the malnutrition and poor health that dogged my grow-ing up in North Korea, I could not keep up with the physical rigors demanded by training for the South Korean police force. I decided instead to study law. It quickly became obvious that I would also need to learn fluent English. I enrolled in an intensive tutoring program in Seoul that matched North Korean defectors with expatriate, English-speaking volunteers. Instead of pairing with just one, I signed up with ten tutors simultaneously! For eight months under their tutelage, I learned about everyone from Shakespeare to the American abolitionist Frederick Douglass, who escaped from slavery. I was enthralled by Douglass's autobiography, and inspired by his letter to his "Old Master," Thomas Auld. It made me wonder what I would write to Kim Jong Un. (His father, Kim Jong Il, had died recently. The former continues to rule North Korea today.) Maybe like Douglass, I thought, I would tell Kim:

> I am myself; you are yourself; we are two distinct persons, equal persons. What you are, I am. You are a human, and so am I. God created both, and made us separate beings. I am not by nature bound to you, nor you to me. Nature does not make your existence depend upon me, or mine to depend upon yours. I cannot walk upon your legs, or you upon mine. I cannot breathe for you, or you for me; I must breathe for myself, and you for yourself. We are distinct persons, and are each equally provided with faculties necessary to our individual existence. In leaving you, I took nothing but what belonged to me . . .

During this time, I was cast on a TV show called *Now On My Way to Meet You*. One of the show's producers had seen me on EBS, South Korea's educational channel, being interviewed about North Korea. *Now On My Way to Meet You* invited North Korean defectors, mostly young women, to share stories about their previous lives and ordeals of escape. I wasn't sure if it was a good idea to go public with mine, but I decided that being on TV might increase the chance of reconnecting with Eunmi. "Maybe she will see the show from somewhere in China and make a getaway to South Korea," I remember telling myself. Alas, it didn't work out that way. But the show did give me something of a public profile in South Korea, and I started to appear in more media outlets to increase awareness about the human costs of the regime to the north.

Over the next few years, I accepted a number of invitations, including one to represent North Korea at the One Young World summit—an annual gathering bringing together youth leaders from all over the world—in Ireland in 2014. The OYW organization had asked the North Korean regime itself to send two representatives, and it responded by providing three. There was only room (or money) for two, but the regime wouldn't accept less than three, because—it believes—two people cannot be trusted to spy on each other. Two might collude to defect. That danger is eliminated with three: A spies on B, B spies on C, and C spies on A. In the end, OYW refused to accept, and decided to invite defectors instead. I got the call and flew to Dublin.

The speech was a particularly emotional one. I was asked to appear in full traditional Korean regalia—a flowing pink and white *hanbok*—and was given a heartfelt introduction by James Chau, a prominent Chinese journalist, who later became a close friend.

In that moment, I felt something inside me begin to thaw. For so many years I'd been forced to harden my emotions, to suppress my feelings, to teach myself to become numb. When I took the stage to give my short speech in front of the 1,300 delegates, guests, and media representatives, I decided not to read from the speech I'd prepared, but to open my heart instead.

"North Korea is an unimaginable country . . ." I began. I told the audience how, when I was a child, my mother taught me not to say anything bad about our lives in the country, even in a whisper, because even the birds and mice were listening to me. I told them that in North Korea, you can be executed for making an unauthorized international phone call. "The day I escaped North Korea," I said, "I saw my mother raped by a Chinese broker who had targeted me." Tears were running down my face. Finally, I explained to them that North Korean refugees are vulnerable in China. "Seventy percent of North Korean women and teenage girls are being victimized [in China]. Sometimes sold for as little as two hundred dollars . . ."

I was later told that the speech had been viewed over one billion times globally, across all internet platforms.

I knew then that I'd crossed an invisible line. The scared, hungry, frightened little girl who hid her innermost thoughts even from the birds and mice was gone. I had to close the book on her, and step into a different life: one dedicated to human rights, and improving the lives of people suffering under tyranny. A life of meaning. A life that would make my father proud.

That life would be lived in America.

PART I
THE UNITED STATES OF CONFUSION

1

⌇

Lost in the Big Apple

Arriving in New York City in November of 2014 was like landing on Mars. I'd been to Tyler, Texas, and Atlanta, Georgia, on mission trips in 2013. But New York was different. It was not just a foreign land, it was its own planet.

I was in New York because I'd been given the opportunity to write a book about my life in North Korea and escape to China. On the taxi ride from John F. Kennedy International Airport, driving along Grand Central Parkway and climbing onto the Robert F. Kennedy Bridge, the Manhattan skyscrapers at night looked both majestic and frightening.

In Seoul I'd been isolated, living in a bubble that comprised only home, school, and the set of *Now On My Way to Meet You*. I came away from my life in South Korea with no greater understanding of how to navigate a modern city than I'd had growing up in Hyesan. Now here I was, twenty-one years old, being ferried across great bridges and tunnels and emerging in a sea of lights, steel, and glass.

I remember thinking that every building looked like it was trying to one-up the next, each striving to reach higher than the ones that came before, as if the city was the very physical embodiment of capitalism—an impression strengthened by the names of the most impressive structures: Rockefeller, Vanderbilt, Chrysler, Woolworth, Trump, Hearst, Carnegie. "The Empire State," read all the black-and-yellow license plates. It was the quintessential American dichotomy, I thought: the limitless grandeur of an empire, the limiting sovereignty of a state.

What a perfect contrast to where I came from! The only majesty, the only grandeur, the only *symbolism* in North Korea is reserved for the cult of a single man: the Supreme Leader. The statues are of him, the monuments are of him, the names of buildings and streets are of him, and the "ideas" or "movements" he sanctioned. Nothing and no one else is allowed to compete for attention, let alone greatness. New York City was the opposite: It was a great game board, where human beings came to compete with each other, each leaving his or her mark in the physical world.

When the taxi dropped me off at my hotel, I realized where I was. Times Square.

Americans scoff when I tell them what it was like for me, because they only associate it with trash, overcrowding, tastelessness, weirdos, and tourism, but for me, Times Square was awe-inspiring. A common refrain from the North Korean regime is that one day it will make the United States "a sea of fire," which successive nuclear blasts will make "glow in the dark." Standing in the middle of Times Square, it seemed to me to be on fire already. At night, the gargantuan LED screens made the street and the faces of other people brighter than in daytime. It was a kind of controlled chaos: The lights danced rhythmically, at regular intervals, as if there were an invisible conductor some-where, luring passersby with clothing, or a Broadway show, or fizzy water, or a pair of golden arches. (These I remembered from Tyler and Seoul—something about a "happy meal.")

The only place in Hyesan with permanent power was the statue of Kim Jong Il in the center square that was illuminated at night. Elsewhere in the city, it was normal to go for weeks and sometimes months without electricity. Candles were very expensive, and battery-powered flashlights scarce. The games I played with friends as a kid were mostly played in the dark. And now here I was, in an ocean of light at night.

IT ALL began after my speech in Dublin at the One Young World con-ference went viral. Later, I was asked by UN Watch, a nonprofit orga-nization, to address the United Nation's 30th Human Rights Council. I felt it was a great honor, and I intended to use the opportunity to bring greater awareness to the oppression of North Koreans by the Kim regime. For reasons that remain unclear, I was seated very close to the staff of the North Korean Permanent Mission to the United Na-tions, which took the opportunity to harass and intimidate me with rude, off-color remarks.

By this point, the regime had already started to spread vicious ru-mors about me and my family. The regime had even put some of my relatives and neighbors on state-sponsored television, forcing them to denounce me with false, vile claims. (These videos ended up and still remain on YouTube, which in the fall of 2020 demonetized my own videos about human rights violations in North Korea. More on that in a later chapter.)

In 2014, before the One Young World conference, I had met Thor Halvorssen, the founder of the Human Rights Foundation, at a "hackathon" the group had sponsored in Silicon Valley to "hack North Korea." While I didn't really understand what hacking was, I had found the experience quite fun, and the friendships I made there enduring. At the Oslo Freedom Forum (OFF) in Norway later that year, I met another friend who told me about a program that the United States immigration system had to attract certain individuals to America. I was intrigued, and through some research, I eventually learned about the O-1 "Extraordinary" visa. I didn't understand much about it, but decided to apply. While I had some limited, touristic experience of life in Texas and Georgia, I didn't think I would ever get to *live* there.

I will never forget the day I received the news that my application had been approved. Not only that, but I was given the chance to become a permanent resident. At the time I'd been reading biographies of America's great civil rights heroes, Martin Luther King Jr. and Rosa Parks, and was feeling particularly inspired. My mind raced with all that I needed to prepare for a successful transition to life in America.

I was quite fond of New York and had friends who lived there, so on a whim, I decided I would make it my home.

My first priority was to continue my education. I had heard repeatedly in South Korea and in my travels that an education at an American university is the best in the world. I was determined to join a top program and learn from the most brilliant minds the country had to offer. I eventually accepted an offer to enroll at Columbia University— an institution I'd heard wonderful things about, with a long list of notable alumni that included Amelia Earhart, Warren Buffett, and the then-president of the United States, Barack Obama. It was with total exhilaration that I stepped on the hallowed ground of Columbia University in January 2016.

BEFORE I was able to begin my new life as a student in America, I first had to come to grips with my new life as a North Korean in America. And many aspects of daily life in New York were an inversion of the only reality I'd ever known.

Nowhere was this more jarring than in the realm of food.

When my parents were imprisoned in hard labor camps, Eunmi and I picked and ate wild greens to avoid starvation. In New York, I noticed that people obsessively ate leaves and paid handsome prices for them in order to lose weight. It was difficult to grasp that people did this because they suffered from or were afraid to develop diseases caused by *overeating*. The very concept of "overabundance" was one that would take me a few more months to understand.

A friend taught me how to read the nutrition labels on food items and to look for the number of calories, carbohydrates, and grams of sugar and protein. Other than sugar, I didn't know what any of these categories meant. All I knew was that my friend was explaining all this by way of trying to get me to stop eating Oreos, my favorite food, because they were "processed," as in "unnatural." To me, natural foods—insects and plants—were not only disgusting, but no amount of them could ever make you full. It was "unnatural" foods that were both delicious and made you feel, if you ate enough of them, that you didn't need to eat anymore. Processed foods like Oreos were clearly win-win. Where was the harm?

During that year when Eunmi and I had to fend for ourselves, we promised each other that if we ever became adults, we would make as much money as we could so that we could eat bread until we were full. We would argue about how much we thought we could eat. She told me she could eat an entire bucket of bread; I said I could eat ten. She would say twenty, I would say *a hundred*. A *mountain* of bread, even!

"A daily meal of meat soup and boiled rice" was what Kim Il Sung had promised during the revolution. For this modest guarantee, Koreans ceded their rights and property to him. Three-quarters of a century later, rice and stew is still a common dying wish for North Koreans; it was one of my father's.

Under the same sky, seven thousand miles away, I was now being educated in "dietary restrictions." One night, I visited a friend in Brooklyn who asked me what mine were. "I don't think I have any," I responded. "What are yours?" "Dairy, nuts, and gluten," she replied. Curious, I asked why. "Food allergies," she said, matter-of-factly. "What are those?" I asked, to her horror. She realized the extent of my ignorance and was kind enough to bring me up to speed, not only on people's medical restrictions—which were understandable enough—but on their *moral* restrictions, which I had a harder time comprehending. It turned out that New York was full of people who didn't consume meat or even non-meat, animal-related food products.

The first several friends I made in New York all had one thing in common: They were all shocked by how much I ate. My favorite food was steak, large, juicy, grilled, nutritious steak. Whether it was a little filet or a massive tomahawk, it didn't matter. There was something magical about them. In North Korea, cows have more rights than people. The lack of private property rights means cows belong not to ranchers but to the regime. Even many cattle ranchers who help raise and tend them are not allowed to eat the meat, which is reserved only for government elites. My mother told me she once witnessed a young man executed in the market in Hyesan for butchering a cow without government permission. In New York, eating meat wasn't just something I enjoyed. With each bite I took, I felt like I was raising a middle finger to the North Korean regime.

A related oddity was the American culture of fitness. I'd heard in South Korea that people in New York are very busy, always in a hurry. When I went to Central Park for the first time, I felt I understood what they meant, because it was true—Americans were literally *running* everywhere. *Where were they all running to?* I wondered. It was only later that I learned they were only running in circles—to "burn calories."

Central Park was at least a very big circle in which people could run. But I discovered that there were small businesses that specialized in providing very small, office-sized circles for people to run in—"gyms." People would take their hard-earned cash, I learned, and spend it on running very fast in a very small space in order to deplete themselves of calories. If there was one thing I'd learned growing up, it was how to *preserve* energy. But these Americans were just giving it away, and not even for free—they were paying for it!

I also found ideas of beauty in America to be amusing and interesting. In North Korea, to be overweight and bald with a large belly is considered attractive. In many places in the third world, in fact, obesity is a status symbol; it indicates wealth and abundance. It's the equivalent of driving a Lamborghini down Park Avenue. But in the United States, everybody wanted to look skinny—like starving North Koreans, I thought. When I saw ads for Victoria's Secret models, it was hard for me to understand how people could consider them beautiful. They all appeared malnourished, the only difference being that they were apparently very tall. (In North Korea, malnourishment and the attendant lack of vitamins and minerals has resulted in millions of people genetically identical to their South Korean neighbors being significantly shorter on average, by as many as three to five inches.)

Physical health aside, Americans also seemed to have an interesting attitude toward *mental* health. One of the first things my agent suggested was to seek out a therapist to treat my "trauma." I didn't understand either concept; I had no words for them in my North Korean dialect (which consisted of only adjectives and synonyms to describe a "socialist paradise" with "nothing to envy." There are no words in North Korean for tyranny, trauma, or depression—or love, for that matter). Without words to describe an emotion or phenomenon, I discovered, it is easy enough to live your life not even knowing they exist. Totalitarian regimes understand this fact quite well.

It was strange to notice that my new friends and colleagues living in conditions of "overabundance" also seemed to have their own versions of "trauma," for which many of them were receiving help from a doctor licensed in therapy. It was so strange, in fact, that I figured I must be in an incredibly good place, being someone who clearly didn't need therapy. Even if I was "traumatized," what would be the point of having survived it only to have to pay someone else to complain to about it, rather than turn it into something positive? Some of my new American friends caught on to my incomprehension and eventually developed a sense of humor about it, later referring to their issues as "first world problems."

The other big surprise was money. Many people I encountered in New York worked in finance—a field that does not exist in North Korea, where there is no financial system, private ownership, or markets. The one thing my father taught me about money was to never, ever go into debt. Despite North Korea's ban on most forms of private ownership and financial transactions, there are a lot of "private lend-ers" who get rich by loaning money on monthly interest.

My parents sometimes borrowed from these loan sharks to keep their business going, but after black-market prices collapsed and a lot of their merchandise was confiscated or stolen, they weren't able to pay back what they borrowed, which was the equivalent of less than two U.S. dollars. Every night, debt collectors came to the house while we were eating our modest supper. They would often yell at my parents in front of me and my sister and threaten them. At a cer-tain point, my father decided he couldn't take it anymore. This was how he'd decided to move into the much riskier venture of smug-gling valuable metals like copper, nickel, and cobalt into China—the decision that was the beginning of the end for us in North Korea. "Yeonmi-ya," he said to me one day, "do not ever borrow money, no matter how hard life gets. Going into debt can take away your dignity."

Finance in America was—like food, fitness, and beauty—a world away. Listening to people passionately discuss investment ideas or the latest Wall Street developments was like trying to follow a conversa-tion in Martian. "What's a private equity fund? What's a hedge fund? A stock?" I learned that in America (and elsewhere around the globe), people bought, sold, and traded things that *did not exist in the physical world*. Now, *that* boggled my mind. In North Korea, everything traded on the black market was concrete, something you could hold in your hands. People exchanged tangible goods for hard cash. That was it. Concepts like ETFs, index funds, and—my God—*Bitcoin* were so far removed from anything I had encountered that I decided the only way I could understand this brave new world around me was to read every-thing I could get my hands on in order to learn.

THEN THERE was race. In North Korea, we are taught that we belong to the Kim Il Sung Race. Growing up, I didn't know that I was *Asian*. I didn't know what Asia was. I was just one of several million descendants of a single man.

In New York, I met Arab Americans, African Americans, European Americans, Asian Americans, and Jewish Americans. I had no clue about the various racial and cultural stereotypes ascribed to the members of each group, no understanding of the nuances within different ethnicities and the historical context for the existence of each. Looking back on it, I was an interesting social science experiment— what happens if you take a twenty-one-year-old blank slate, to whom all concepts of race and racism are completely foreign, and drop her in New York City?

From where I sat, America seemed to be the melting pot of legend: all different types of people living, working, interacting, loving, and just existing side by side. It was beautiful! But this was to be the beginning of a long and difficult education, which I discuss in greater detail in later chapters.

Not having eyes or ears for the racial tensions I'd later learn about, one thing that stood out to me instead during my early months in America was the compassion and inclusiveness that people showed toward those with disabilities. As a child in rural North Korea, I saw many people who had been exiled from Pyongyang after having suffered debilitating, irreversible injuries while working for the state. The regime shamed these people with the term "sickened-body," and relegated them to the countryside to starve. The authorities would also regularly detain people with congenital conditions like dwarfism, put them in camps, and sterilize them to filter them out of the gene pool.

In America, I noticed that sidewalks were cut to accommodate people in wheelchairs, ramps and elevators accompanied stairs in every building, and special accommodations were built into everything from restrooms to public transportation. I later learned that this was the legacy of the Americans with Disabilities Act, passed by Congress in 1990.

What an unbelievable idea, I thought: At a certain point, Americans with disabilities and elderly infirmities took it upon themselves to develop civic associations, lobby their elected representatives, and convince their fellow citizens to set aside hard-earned tax revenue to make life easier on those who have a harder time getting around. They did it, and from what I can tell, it is now a completely uncontroversial decision. It was simply amazing.

This one, narrow area of life—accommodations for people with disabilities—came to represent everything that I was learning to love about America: democracy, self-determination, civic participation, entrepreneurship, solidarity, and compassion.

It was everything that my teachers and peers at Columbia would spend the next four years trying to convince me were lies.

2

The Fall of Lady Columbia

More than the lights and skyscrapers, more than the bridges and rivers, the Columbia University campus in Morningside Heights on Manhattan's Upper West Side was the most breathtaking sight I'd ever seen. Coming from Seoul, everything in New York seemed majestic to me, but the beauty of Columbia was of a different order of magnitude. Walking around campus, I felt an overwhelming intimidation. Navigating the massive labyrinth of quads and buildings, I frequently went slack-jawed, my mouth agape, and had to remind myself to close it. Columbia doesn't have tall skyscrapers like downtown Manhattan, but the grandeur of the campus made me feel equally small.

The exception was the Low Memorial Library, with the bronze statue of Alma Mater in front. Looking down on me with welcoming arms, she seemed to be inviting me to take part in something larger than myself, to make myself at home—to feel like I belonged here.

As an eight-year-old girl visiting Pyongyang, the gargantuan bronze statues of Kim Il Sung and Kim Jong Il—the Mansu Hill Grand Monument—made me feel frightened, as they are intended to do. Looking up at Alma Mater's beautifully shaped face, kind eyes, and inviting arms, I felt safe. I would come to think of her, if only symbolically, as my new "nurturing mother."

Columbia is one of the few institutions in America that is older than the country itself. Established in 1754, it predates the Declaration of Independence by twenty-two years, and the Constitution by thirty-three. It was originally called King's College, established by royal charter under King George II, and housed on the grounds of Trinity Church. As I soon learned, the name change occurred in 1784, after the American Revolutionary War. Alexander Hamilton and John Jay, who sat on the university's board of trustees at the time, were instrumental in changing its name to Columbia. Many people think Columbia simply means "pertaining to Christopher Columbus," but that is incomplete at best.

Lady Columbia is a national personification of the United States of America, the female counterpart to Uncle Sam. The typical depiction is of a beautiful young woman with outstretched arms or holding a bright torch, lighting the way toward the promised land. Paintings usually depict a stern face with a faint, knowing smile. She is simultaneously confident and comforting, an American Mona Lisa.

The symbol of a beautiful woman raising an arm in defiance is ubiquitous in revolutionary art. The image of Marianne or Liberty hoisting the flag and leading soldiers over the barricades is one of the most iconic of the French Revolution, and survives in personifications of the French Republic to this day. "Mother Russia" was used by the anti-Bolshevik White movement in the Russian Civil War, and by the Bolsheviks in the war against Hitler. For 137 years, immigrants to America have waited with bated breath to glimpse a rusted copper statue of the robed goddess of liberty looming in Upper New York Bay.

My favorite Lady Columbia cameo is not in a painting or statue, however, but in a poem by Phillis Wheatley. Written during the Revolutionary War in 1776, Wheatley's poem, "His Excellency General Washington," captured the essence of Columbia and her role as a symbol of power, hope, and liberty:

> *One century scarce performed its destined round,*
> *When Gallic powers Columbia's fury found;*
> *And so may you, whoever dares disgrace*
> *The land of freedom's heaven-defended race!*
> *Fix'd are the eyes of nations on the scales,*
> *For in their hopes Columbia's arm prevails*

Wheatley was born in West Africa in 1753, sold into slavery in Boston, and eventually became the first African American to ever publish a book of poetry, bringing her recognition in both London and the North American colonies. The publication of her book convinced her masters to free her, but at age thirty-one, after having lost three children, she died poor and forgotten.

There are many such stories throughout American history, featuring lives full of immense contradiction: misery and triumph, oppression and emancipation, failure and success, evil and good, all existing side by side, in parallel, as they do in every human heart. It is the genius of America that the literary talent and brilliance of a West African slave was ever discovered in the first place; it is the tragedy of America that she was destroyed by the conditions to which it subjected her. It is impossible to understand American history or the American character without facing both truths head on—a reality that Columbia University, to my astonishment, would try its best to suppress.

IT WAS orientation day, and I couldn't have been more excited. What an unbelievable honor to start my studies as an Ivy League student! Having witnessed firsthand the yawning gap between communist ideology and economic reality in North Korea, the separation of rural China from the country's city-based economic growth, and the capitalist miracle in South Korea, I had already decided to pursue a degree in economics. In addition to courses in their majors, all Columbia students are required to take the college's "core" classes: a comprehensive liberal arts education designed to cover the full spectrum of history, science, art, and the humanities. It was a dream come not quite true.

During the first day of orientation, an instructor from the general studies department asked a group of freshmen and transfer students if any of us had read and liked Jane Austen. I raised my hand eagerly, and said in my still somewhat broken English that I found her characters—created two centuries earlier—to be instantly relatable. "Wrong," the instructor said. "Those books promote female oppression, racism, colonialism, and white supremacy." I wasn't angry or even confused. I just assumed that I *must* have misunderstood her. My comprehension abilities were by no means perfect, and I just resolved to ask one of my new classmates later on what the professor had actually said. But "Jane Austen books," the professor clearly went on, "propagate the idea that women are inferior to men; that only white males are fully evolved and capable of higher-level thinking; that salvation is only achievable through the dogma of Christianity." She continued by informing us that Austen, like all white writers during the colonial era, supported white supremacy and racism. She ended with a line I'll never forget: "This is how we look for hidden systemic racism and oppression."

As a student in Hyesan, our teachers often reminded us that we must vigilantly look for *hidden signs* of infiltration by our enemies—American Bastards causing, stoking, and lurking behind all of our problems. Food was scarce, the lights went out, and our parents were disappeared in the middle of the night because of American Bastards. You might not see or hear them, but the American Bastards were every-where, perhaps even in the air we breathed.

One of the core classes I was most excited to attend was Master-pieces of Western Music. In South Korea I'd discovered Beethoven and Chopin, and loved the piano sonatas the most. Beethoven's music in particular was so intense and powerful, I felt a certain sense of transcendence listening to it, as millions of people all over the world have for the last two hundred years. I had learned that Beethoven was a transitional figure between the Classical and Romantic periods of Western music, and wondered what it could mean that lyricless music could be considered "romantic." In North Korea, of course, the state has attempted to annihilate the very concept of romance, as the only type of love it sanctions is that between the people and their Dear Leader. Romance between couples I'd come to understand mostly through pirated films and television series, but in *music*? I was excited to learn.

During the orientation session for Masterpieces of Western Music, a department lecturer asked who among the students might have a problem with studying "Western Music." Chastened by the Jane Aus-ten experience, I was slightly less stupefied when every single one of my peers in the room raised their hand, seemingly in unison. But I was still confused: Was everyone objecting to the music itself, or to the people who composed it, or to the term *Western*—or maybe to the word *music*? Who knew?! The lecturer called on one of the students to explain why. The student said that white men in Europe and America had silenced and excluded the composers and musicians of color, so it made no sense to refer to Western music or a "Western canon," only a "white canon." The lecturer agreed, and added that he had no control over the core curriculum.

I was still feeling intimidated and a bit meek in these hallowed classrooms, but by this point I was feeling a little annoyed, and raised my hand. I ventured to say that I thought it was okay to call them Western musicians if that's how they thought of themselves at the time, and in any case, we could maybe also learn about their musical genius in addition to whatever troubled times they lived in and the complicated lives they led. The professor responded to this benign statement made in broken English by a young girl who was clearly a recent immigrant by telling me, in front of all my new classmates, that I had likely been "brainwashed." I wanted to cry—not out of sadness or fear or even embarrassment, but from frustration.

The frustration would continue. In a course on human rights, our teacher, a PhD candidate, taught us that because men are inherently violent by nature, "toxic masculinity" imbues nearly all of their actions and relationships and the institutions they run. The professor even used holding doors open for women as an example of the way men use power and violence to signal to women who is really in control.

What a load of crap, I thought to myself, now I was really getting irked. I raised my hand and told the professor that I, a woman, held doors open for both men *and* women, not because I wanted to over-power them, but because my parents taught me that it was polite. I also said that of all the ways in which men *do* use physical superiority to control and subdue women, holding doors open was probably not among them. The professor listened intently as I spoke, and responded by telling me that—as a newcomer to this country—I probably hadn't yet learned the nuances and subtleties of gender interactions in a new culture. I then tried to reduce the discussion to something we couldn't possibly disagree about: I pointed out that because of biological differ-ences, most men, of course, can carry more weight than I can, being eighty pounds and five foot two. She responded that my lack of belief in my own physical equality with men was the result of brainwashing by a sexist culture, and again, that I hadn't learned the nuances of gender relations in the United States.

She was actually right, in a way. Up until that point, I'd only used my own eyes and common sense to conclude that, by and large, men and women are equal but dissimilar: that men were better at carrying heavy things, better at spending time alone, and more interested in ideas; that women were better at multitasking, better at working in teams, and more interested in people. Many exceptions of course exist, but studies generally show that women are in fact better than men, by and large, at verbal fluency, perceptual speed, accuracy, and fine motor skills, while men outperform women in spatial awareness, working memory, and mathematical skills.

What I hadn't learned were "the nuances and subtleties of gender interactions in a new culture: in academia." And these *must*, in fact, be learned, because none of them are intuitive or obvious. The profes-sor asked me where I learned that I couldn't carry as many bricks as a man. I said I weighed eighty pounds, which I did, and left it at that.

IN THE four years I ended up spending at Columbia, professors in the humanities frequently challenged us to demonstrate how woke we were. We had to be diligent in being woke—learning to locate the white male Bastards behind every crime, beneath every problem, in the air we breathed—otherwise we were no better than those who intentionally perpetuate social injustices. Luckily for receptive students, it was easy work. The questions were always predictable, the answers always prefabricated. Students were expected to repeat teachings, not to explain material. We were to memorize and recite, not to grapple or understand. The difference between a passing grade and a stellar one was not accuracy or creativity, but passion and intensity. The difference between a passing grade and a failing one lay in a refusal to criticize the usual targets (capitalism, Western civilization, white supremacy, systemic racism, oppression of minorities, colonialism, etc.). Worse than a bad grade was to be labeled by one's classmates as a "SIX HIRB": a sexist, intolerant, xenophobic, homophobic, Islamophobic, racist bigot.

As a very young student in North Korea, I vividly recall a teacher asking us to solve 1 + 1. I was a bad student from the beginning, so I was proud to finally know the answer to a question: "Two!" I said. "Wrong," the teacher said. She then explained one of the great teachings of our Dear Leader. When he was a small child, like us, Kim Jong Il became the first human being in history to discover an ultimate truth about the universe: that mathematics were made up. He said that if you combine one drop of water with another drop of water, you don't get two drops of water—you get one big drop.

The Dear Leader's harrowing insight has two points. The first is to teach children early on to accept something so obviously idiotic and untrue as nevertheless being a fact. (Not even a child can be convinced that the sum of two sticks is just a big stick, but you can frighten her into shutting up about it.) The second is to teach children that they are not individuals. One person plus one person does not equal two people; 21 million people do not make a society. In North Korea, the only number is one: one leader, followed by one people.

I can already hear my American friends' eyes rolling into the backs of their heads, but I ask you, dear reader, how much *more* insane is all that than what they teach eighteen-year-olds in the Ivy League? We were taught that gender is a societal construct imposed by white men; that science and math itself were also invented by white men to further the agenda of white supremacy; that the goal of technology was not the improvement of life or to push the limits of human knowledge and abilities for its own sake, but as a means of imprisoning the masses by elites; and that Christianity, a religion born in the Middle Eastern desert, was the religion of white people, used for no other purpose than to indoctrinate the indigenous tribes they conquered through the use of technology (in the truest sign of stupidity, smallpox *wasn't* mentioned).

It was hard not to think of the persecution of Christianity and all religions in North Korea, where communist fundamentalism considers religion to be the "opiate of the masses" (in the terminology of Karl Marx), and where the Kim family has cribbed the central narrative of Christianity for its own narrow political purposes: Kim Il Sung is God, *the father*, who gave us his son, Kim Jong Il, the Christ.

It was all shaping up to be a pretty disappointing experience, to say the least. How could one of the leading universities in the greatest country in the world teach its students to hate their fellow countrymen? What is the motive behind this destructive narrative? Isn't an American university's mission to train analytically minded individuals capable of civility, constructive social interaction, and open discourse?

One thing was for certain—this was going to be a *long* four years.

3

The Illusion of Safe Space

The contemporary classroom is a product of a bygone era, when the primary purpose of education was to prepare children and teens for adult life in an industrial society. Dozens of students, often uninformed, seated at identical desks, placed at equal distances, and all facing the same direction in order to receive the same instruction from the same individual at the same times every day: This wildly unnatural arrangement made sense in the early part of the twentieth century because young people really did need to be shaped for entrance into a mass, commercial society and for jobs in factories or in clerical work.

But at the same time this setup was used in the United States and elsewhere across the Western world to facilitate participation in industrial, capitalist, democratic societies, it also proved ideal for the political and ideological indoctrination programs of dictatorships. Even in democracies, the classroom provides a captive audience of impressionable minds to a state-sanctioned hierarchy, from which information flows in only one direction. Students are expected to receive ideas, not to wrestle or come up with them, and to internalize what they learn there for the remainder of their adult lives. When students sit patiently as "learnings" are dictated to them, and they're asked to memorize and regurgitate them by rote, it doesn't strike us as odd so long as the "learnings" are in math, biology, English, or American history. But all you have to do is change the material itself to "Kim Il Sung Thought," and you can see the problem.

In the West, the problem has traditionally been avoided by remaining committed to the broad educational values of the Enlightenment. During the rocky course of the Enlightenment in the eighteenth century, primary schools and universities reintroduced a revolutionary idea: critical thinking. This was indeed a reintroduction, not an invention, as the Socratic method of teaching by asking questions and learning by pooling together different answers from different people was already thousands of years old. When Europe fell into the dark ages of dogma and superstition, Muslim scholars were the torchbearers of Socratic education. But the West was eventually to have a rebirth.

Inspired by the ideals of the Renaissance, thinkers of the French school like Voltaire, Pierre Bayle, and Denis Diderot started from the premise that the human mind, when disciplined by reason, is the best vehicle for understanding the nature of the world. Above all, like Plato and Socrates, they valued *intellectual exchange*, in which all views—even those of the so-called authorities—were subjected to serious analysis and painstaking, critical interrogation. They believed that only through such rigorous questioning could ideas with merit surface, and the flaws be uncovered for all to see. Sunlight, in other words, was seen as the greatest disinfectant.

How many parents in America today can recognize that tradition of critical thinking in their children's classrooms? In many American schools and universities, it is no longer acceptable to allow different ideas to compete with or openly challenge one another. Disfavored speakers are often haggled, ridiculed, and silenced during educational events, to the point that many schools have started to cancel appearances by guest speakers and lecturers for fear of safety and security breaches—a development that smacks of the Dark Ages.

I've come to appreciate how much ordinary Americans love and revere the First Amendment to the U.S. Constitution, but perhaps it's difficult for people born here to understand just how radical an idea it really is: *Congress shall make no law respecting an establishment of religion, or prohibiting the free exercise thereof; or abridging the freedom of speech, or of the press; or the right of the people peaceably to assemble, and to petition the Government for a redress of grievances.*

For a refugee from a country like North Korea, that sentence is the very heart of freedom, a prism of cultural and political achievement, the likes of which I never thought possible for human beings not only to write on paper, but to make the very law under which hundreds of millions of individuals would live.

It is a law that Columbia University teaches its students to hate—sometimes subconsciously, sometimes overtly.

ASIDE FROM the Jane Austen incident, there was another landmark moment for me during orientation at Columbia. In the name of helping incoming students "assimilate" to life at the university, faculty and administrators went around the room and told us about Columbia's body of policies—the student Code of Conduct. The school's promotional materials boast about producing well-rounded intellectuals, but there was nothing about that here. There was only a laser-like focus on one goal: keeping the classroom a "safe space."

I was confused. I knew that New York City had a past reputation for violent crime, but the Columbia University campus, dorms, and associated buildings and residential apartments struck me as eminently safe, and Morningside Heights as a perfectly pleasant neighborhood. I quickly realized, however, that by "safe" the instructors were not referring to literal *physical* safety (even though the word *literal* was incorrectly employed several times), but to the apparent right of all students not to feel *emotionally* or *psychologically* injured. The threat of emotional harm was referred to by multiple instructors in order to implicitly explain—in so many words—why classrooms at Columbia do not allow the Socratic method.

Columbia's Code of Conduct reminded me of the seven commandments in George Orwell's *Animal Farm*, which the animals would recite mindlessly, not knowing what they meant exactly or what the consequences would be:

> *Whatever goes upon two legs is an enemy.*
> *Whatever goes upon four legs, or has wings, is a friend.*
> *No animal shall wear clothes.*
> *No animal shall sleep in a bed.*
> *No animal shall drink alcohol.*
> *No animal shall kill any other animal.*
> *All animals are equal.*

Surprised, a little offended, and most of all bored out of my mind, I spent most of the rest of the "safe space" orientation course imagining Orwellian commandments for my new school:

Whatever disagrees, or is silent, is an enemy.

Whatever agrees is a friend.

No student shall speak offenses.

No student shall touch another student.

No student shall make another student feel unsafe.

No student shall speak well of America.

Only white men are free.

It was amusing, but still, I was incredibly paranoid about the possibility of making a fellow student feel unsafe and getting expelled. The terms seemed so vague, and the Code did little to shed light on them. If any word or action could cause someone else discomfort, and if discomfort was grounds for possible disciplinary action, how could I anticipate who would be upset by what, not knowing who anyone was or what they thought?

The orientation on the Code was followed by a series of "consent workshops" (attendance was mandatory), in which we watched videos and sat through lengthy lectures about sex between legal adults. Considering what my mother and I had been through in China, I was initially optimistic about this portion of the orientation, and actually quite touched that Columbia went to such lengths to ensure the *physical* safety of its students. My sense of gratitude was cut short, however, when the instructors described the following scenario: Two students who go out on a date together imbibe alcohol and verbally agree to become intimate, which they do. The next day, the woman accuses the man of rape because, under the influence of alcohol, the consent she gave was not legitimate. So, the instructors asked us, is this an example of rape?

Something tells me you already know their answer, and how insulting I found it.

AS FRESHMAN year wore on, and I took more classes, and progressed in my education, things got weirder. On one particular occasion, a professor sent students an email warning them that if a certain aspect of reading assignments triggered painful memories or uncomfortable feelings, they would not be expected to complete the assignments. "Don't even come to class," the email continued, "and don't feel obligated to explain why you were triggered." New policies announced that emotional support animals were henceforth to be allowed on campus, and even encouraged inside classrooms. I remember someone's dog licking my shoes during one lecture, and not knowing what to do besides laugh.

Professors and administrators spoke to us like children, and so many students acted accordingly. People my age and literally double my size, who appeared to be incredibly fit and well-fed, were sometimes reduced to tears discussing feelings they harbored that appeared to have no possible connection to anything we were supposed to be learning about. A lecture on Homer would end with a white student crying about colonialism. A class on government would take the form of two students trying to outdo each other as LGBTQ allies. In the months I spent studying criminal justice in South Korea, I never learned that injustices could be fought by spinning new ones out of thin air.

In reality, of course, Columbia's "safe space" was elite code language for restrictions on ideological heterogeneity. I had imagined Columbia to be a marketplace of ideas, where students had unlimited possibilities to think differently and push the boundaries of the status quo, creating a better future. A "safe space" in this context presumably would mean a place where ideas could be expressed without fear of reprisal. Instead, it meant a place where—to invert the phrase popularized by Ben Shapiro—feelings don't care about your facts. I started to despair that my new institutional home would not be a vehicle to search for truth, but the opposite: a cult.

That word might sound like an exaggeration, but consider that on the first day of most courses, professors asked us to introduce ourselves by stating not only our names and where we came from but our pronouns. I knew what a pronoun was grammatically, but couldn't for the life of me figure out what it meant that each of us possessed a preferred one. In the English classes I had taken in South Korea, the list of personal pronouns included the subjective *I, you, he, she, it, we,* and *they,* the objective counterparts *me, you, him, her, it, us,* and *them,* and the possessive forms *mine, your/yours, his, her/hers, its, our/ours,* and *their/theirs.* Personal pronouns were used in statements and commands, but not in questions; interrogative pronouns (like *who, whom,* and *what*) were used for that purpose. These lessons were fresh in my memory, and I could still rattle them off.

But my South Korean tutors were apparently quite backward, employing English grammatical rules that merely existed from about 1450 to 2014, and hadn't gotten the memo: There are, in fact, *seventy-eight gender pronouns.* Some, like *Zie/Ze,* sounded to me like Americans doing bad impressions of Germans, an odd preference; others, like *Ver/Vis,* were reminiscent of tongue twisters in Latin class. My personal favorites were *Xe/Xem* and *Xyr,* which looked and sounded like they came from Mendeleev's periodic table of elements. Most bore no resemblance to anything in the rest of the English language. I was already struggling to master my new language and felt quite insecure about it. Now I ran the risk of offending my peers by misstating their pronouns, no matter how hard I tried to remember them. As if these dynamics weren't confusing enough, these pronouns could not even be guessed at simply by observing the phenotypic appearance of my classmates.

I'll never forget one classmate, a biological male who identified as gender fluid and preferred *they/their*, taking offense when I accidentally used *he*. I made grammatical mistakes all the time, something that was obvious to all of my classmates, who were always too polite to correct me, as I was clearly a recent immigrant. But not this classmate, who upbraided me after class. I wanted to tell this fragile soul about life in North Korea versus life in America, but of course I didn't. In fact, in the student's eyes I could see real suffering. They weren't faking it; they were in pain. They truly felt threatened, harmed, and oppressed. I actually sympathized. I remembered as a child being so brainwashed by my teachers that I sincerely believed the Dear Leader could read my mind. Even in China, after my escape from North Korea, I still believed this. It was only after arriving in South Korea that I learned that the Kims were not gods, and that they had no ability to see my thoughts.

I mean it when I say that all I felt for this person was compassion, empathy, and understanding. I couldn't blame them for being so severed from reality that they felt entitled to talk to me as if I were a bigot, when I was just a very recent immigrant who made a mistake that, according to what I'd been taught, wasn't actually a mistake. This person was simply lost, completely untethered from life, with no sense whatsoever of what either justice or injustice meant or looked like. And it probably wasn't even their fault.

Years later, in 2019, when I delivered a TED Talk in Vancouver, I chose to speak on this topic. Many people think that human beings inherently know and understand justice and injustice, that we're each innately born with a robust ethical conscience that can clearly identify what is right and what is wrong. I believe this is nonsense.

All it takes is a quick scan of history to understand that the human experience has been mostly defined by violence, crime, starvation, and oppression. Concepts of justice are not inherent to highly evolved primates, they are unique and precarious achievements of human civilization. Acquiescence to slavery is the default human setting. Without the Enlightenment, there would have been no counter-default movement for abolition.

When I lived in North Korea, I was brainwashed to believe that the Kims were starving just like us, simply because that's what I was taught from a young age. It wasn't until a friend in South Korea pointed out to me that Kim Jong Il had a big, round belly that I realized he couldn't possibly be starving. Quite literally, I had to be *taught* to use *reason* to deduce that Kim Jong Il was in fact fat, even though a baby could have seen it.

That's why the subversion of critical thinking is so dangerous. It is the mechanism by which humans lose their faculties as individuals and succumb to groupthink, which is a precondition for every totalitarian society on Earth, and which ultimately felled my father.

THROUGHOUT MY twenty-nine years on Earth, one thing I have come to appreciate about the world is its unknowable complexity. The U.S. military has an acronym for it, in fact: VUCA stands for volatility, uncertainty, complexity, and ambiguity. Originally used to describe the conditions of the post–Cold War world, VUCA is a stand-in for all factors that lead to human uncertainty and unease. Especially in the modern era, the complexity and uncertainty of everyday life is so high that most people cannot begin to understand it, nor do they want to try—it's simply too overwhelming.

Tyrannical regimes understand the confusion of life under VUCA. Their first task is to *simplify* life for their subjects, often through a fictional narrative. In North Korea, for example, how could a people and a land practically identical to prosperous and well-fed South Korea possibly suffer periodic famines and mass malnutrition? Well, because of the American Bastards, you see, who want us to suffer; but lucky for us, we are only alive in the first place because of our Dear Leader, who makes sure we have nothing to envy.

In my more generous and kindhearted moments, I could see that many of my fellow students at Columbia were suffering under their own version of VUCA: The 2008 financial crisis was still in recent memory, the job market was uncertain, and a BA wasn't worth what it was in the past. New York is a busy and sometimes scary place, crime is high, and living conditions aren't always comfortable. And sure, exams are stressful, studying is difficult, and cramming deprives you of sleep. It's a complex world out there! But instead of girding us for an even more volatile world outside the confines of an Ivy League campus and trying to instill us with some backbone and fortitude, Columbia professors seemed to be primarily engaged in their own version of autocratic simplification: Feel tired, stressed, and a little frightened of the future? It's because the system is rigged against you. It was built by white men in order to subjugate you. Only by destroying that system will you finally find peace, security, and confidence.

It went on like this for four years.

Columbia University's motto is "*In Lumine Tuo Videbimus Lumen*"; it is a Latin phrase borrowed from the book of Psalms (36:9) meaning, "In Thy light shall we see light." But the Columbia I knew saw no light at all, in the world or in people. It saw only darkness, which I knew to be a lie.

4

Hypocrisy of the Elite

I n 1958, British sociologist and politician Michael Young wrote *The Rise of the Meritocracy*, which has since become a classic. A reaction to the postwar tripartite system of public education, Young's satire described a dystopian United Kingdom in which "merit" replaced class as the primary means of division and created a society made up of a powerful elite, on the one hand, and a powerless underclass on the other. The book is commonly misread as an attack on merit, rather than a prophecy of a class of educated, technocratic elites who seize power and wield it at the expense of ordinary people, who can never hope to join their ranks.

In the last few years, I've had the opportunity to meet many of America's elites. I was initially very humbled by the invitations I received from wealthy and influential people to speak at events or to discuss my life and activism after my One Young World speech in Dublin just happened to go viral. These invitations seemed to come early and often, many times from names I was later shocked and embarrassed not to have recognized.

In October of 2014, I was still at the Oslo Freedom Forum when I received an invitation from some guy named Jeff Bezos from a company called Amazon. I had never heard of either, and so I replied that I was going to be busy (even though I wasn't!). I was also invited to speak at several conferences, including Women in the World hosted by Tina Brown, the founding editor-in-chief of the *Daily Beast*. At Women in the World, I was scheduled to speak right before Hillary Rodham Clinton—a name I *was* familiar with from news coverage in South Korea when she was secretary of state. Other speakers there included Jon Stewart of *The Daily Show*, the famous actress Meryl Streep, and other political figures like Samantha Power, then America's ambassador to the United Nations.

This conference was a watershed moment for me and my understanding of the world. Until that point, I thought that the international community had neglected to do anything for the North Korean people because they *didn't know what was going on there*. After all, only about two hundred North Korean defectors have made it to America legally in the past seventy-plus years, and no one inside North Korea can communicate with the outside world. After accepting the invitation to speak at the conference, I resolved to use the opportunity to share with the esteemed audience what was actually going on in North Korea, so that Americans and Europeans with real money, power, and influence would feel inspired and empowered to do something. At the very least, I was sure that they would help spread the word about the modern-day holocaust taking place in North Korea, about the fact that it is being aided and abetted by the Chinese Communist Party, and that tens and even hundreds of thousands of mostly female

North Korean defectors are being sold, raped, and otherwise harmed in China.

In a word, that isn't what happened. It turned out that the purpose of a conference like Women in the World was not to mobilize financial capital and political power among people who are fortunate enough to possess it in order to help people suffering in places like China and North Korea; it was—if there was any point at all—to passionately discuss the suffering of women *in America*. The word *oppression* here was defined to mean things like making ninety cents on the dollar compared with men, or being only the vice president of a Fortune 500 company rather than the CEO, or how male-dominated office culture doesn't make it safe for women to cry. As much as I tried to have compassion, I again couldn't believe what I was hearing.

Hillary Clinton watched my speech from the greenroom backstage, since she was the next speaker after me. It was October of 2015 and she was running for president at the time. I remember she wore a black-and-white jacket that made her look like former German chancellor Angela Merkel, but was also faintly reminiscent of Kim Jong Il's trademark winter parka. When I came down from the stage in tears after my speech, Clinton came up to me, looked me in the eye, and told me that she would never forget what I said that day. She promised that she would do everything in her power to help the women of North Korea.

Perhaps she might have if she'd been elected president; I doubt it. But with her political ambitions thwarted the following year, and, you'd think, nothing to do but administer the massive funds of the nonprofit Clinton Foundation and use her considerable personal fame and power for good, she elected instead to spend the next several years—as far as I could tell—complaining about not being president. Ever since, I've never seen her mention the atrocities suffered by North Korean women. Not even once.

AS IT was for so many other Americans, the election of 2016 was another milestone in my understanding of the world. From the time I arrived in New York, I'd tried to consume as much American news coverage as possible, both because it helped improve my English abilities and because I thought it would keep me informed about my new country and the wider world. Being a recent Manhattanite, I decided to read the *New York Times* and the *Washington Post* every day in Columbia's Butler Library and listen to National Public Radio in my dorm.

As recently as the previous year, I had no opinion of any of the Republican or Democratic candidates for president, nor did I think one way or the other about the parties in general. Americans seemed to think that the GOP and Democrats were like Mars and Venus, but to me they seemed, if not necessarily identical, then at least more similar to each other than either of them were to anything I knew from Korea or China. But by Election Day of 2016, I was, in my own naive way, radicalized. I was convinced that Donald Trump was a fascist, a would-be dictator, and a rapist. I told my fiancé at the time (whose companionship and role in my life I explain in a later chapter) that if he had any reasons for liking Trump, I didn't want to hear them, and that if he even considered voting for Trump, I wouldn't marry him. Some of my girlfriends in Brooklyn and Manhattan would go to weeknight meetings to organize efforts for how to resist Trump and how we could bring him down. When they told me about their plans to move to Canada if Clinton lost, I believed them.

Looking back on it, I didn't know a single American at the time who supported Trump, or even anybody who just felt neutral about the election. My peers were all very smart people, had much higher levels of educational attainment than I did, and had spent far more of their lives in the United States than I had. Everything I absorbed from them was mutually reinforced by everything I read in the newspapers and everything I heard on the radio. When I saw Trump's face or heard his voice and felt viscerally angry, there was simply no reason to think twice about where on earth these feelings were coming from.

I still remember the moment when my fiancé called and told me that Trump had won. I was in my bed and felt afraid. I started to sob. I called my friends to see how they were doing, and they checked in on me. I watched cable news all day, read through the major national newspapers, and listened to radio and podcasts. It was clear that Trump had colluded with the Russians to steal the election from Clinton, and also that he would soon be impeached and removed from office, if not assassinated. If not, then the dark night of fascism would soon fall on America, the place I'd immigrated to in search of freedom. It was just my luck that I'd finally arrived here only in time to watch it disintegrate into the kind of dictatorship from which I'd escaped.

This was now the world I inhabited: one in which a single election victory by one of America's two political parties spelled the end of the Republic, the death of peace and freedom, the end of the line. This was the world of the *New York Times*, the *Washington Post*, NPR, and Columbia—the world of the elite.

It took a long time for me to start thinking for myself, rather than within the boundaries set for me. For the first fourteen years of my life, which is when we learn how to think, there was no thinking for me to do. What kind of haircut should I get? That was a decision made only by the regime. What kind of music should I listen to? The regime decided for us. What kinds of books and movies? The regime, again. There was no opportunity to develop critical human faculties like judgment, imagination, or taste, which of course is the objective of every dictatorial regime. North Korea is so successful in this respect that once I was finally free in South Korea, I was crippled by the expectation and even the thought that I had to actually make decisions and think for myself. Which jeans should I wear? I wished someone else would pick for me. Where should I eat dinner? Can't someone else decide? In the first several months I lived in Seoul, I felt overwhelmed even by small, meaningless decisions like these—so much so that at one point, I remember thinking that if I could be guaranteed a supply of frozen potatoes and an exemption from execution for having defected, I'd like to go back to North Korea.

It was not the education I received at Columbia, or following the American press, that helped me finally break out of this habit. It was reading old books. Michael Young's *The Rise of the Meritocracy* was one; George Orwell's collected writings were another. I started to believe, as I still do now, that the only way to think for yourself is to ignore the mainstream media, and largely forget the daily news cycle, and connect instead with the great minds of the past, who know all of our problems better than we do ourselves. There is a reason why the great books of Western civilization are all banned in dictatorships.

Before my father's arrest, when I was seven or eight years old, I remember that one night in our home, he was sitting with a small glass bottle with cooking oil and a cotton thread inside, which he ignited with a lighter to turn it into a reading lamp. My father was holding a bundle of bound pages with no front or back cover. When I asked him what it was, he said it was part of a book about North Korean soldiers that were captured by the South during the Korean War. I remember him telling me then that the benefit of reading books, if you could find them, was that you could learn common sense, which you don't get taught in classrooms, because they are filled with propaganda.

IN MARCH of 2016, I'd received another speaking invitation, this time to something called "Campfire." Once a year or so, Jeff Bezos (who by this time I knew was the founder and CEO of Amazon, and that this was a large company indeed!) brings together a small group of famous and successful writers, artists, musicians, and filmmakers for an exclusive, off-the-record weekend of relaxation, socializing, and storytelling by fascinating people who have lived extraordinary lives. Previous guests included (in no particular order) Neil Armstrong, Bette Midler, Walter Mosley, Neil Gaiman, Robert Sapolsky, Tom Hanks, Ron Howard, and Billie Jean King. The event that year would be held from September 29 to October 2 at the Biltmore Hotel in Santa Barbara, California. Guests were asked to prepare twenty-five-minute speeches to be delivered to an audience of 150 other notable guests.

I was taking classes while continuing my human rights advocacy work at the time, and I took the week off to attend Campfire. Bezos sent a Gulfstream private jet to New York to pick up several attendees, including me. I boarded the plane with famous actors and writers whose names I don't recall, but I do remember one guest, who introduced himself as Harvey Weinstein. I had no clue who he was, but my fiancé told me that he was a very famous film producer.

It was, naturally enough, my first time on a private jet, and I'd never seen such a beautiful plane in my life. At the private airport we departed from, there was no security or baggage check. It was a sunny but chilly day, and I came straight from a morning class at Columbia.

By this time I'd learned more about Jeff Bezos, who was evidently not just the CEO of Amazon but one of the wealthiest and most powerful people on the face of the earth. I boarded his plane with the same hope I harbored taking the stage at the Women in the World conference: I was confident that with his help, I was going to find a way to improve the lot of North Koreans—if not the ones trapped in the country itself then at least some of the 300,000 defectors in China, where I'd heard Bezos did a lot of his business. In my view, it wouldn't take much; the mere *acknowledgment* of what was happening to my people in China by someone like Bezos might have a ripple effect, convincing other American investors to put pressure on Beijing to reduce its support for Pyongyang.

This was, of course, before I'd learned that the power dynamic goes the other way around: that American investors and business-people are far more dependent on the Chinese market than the Chinese government is on them. Even Jeff Bezos, the world's wealthiest man, made his billions by building a company that—whatever its other merits and considerable achievements—essentially serves as a storefront for Chinese sellers and products. Bezos, it turned out, also owned the *Washington Post*. Go figure.

It was with high hopes that I embarked on the Gulfstream. Other people boarded the plane in a timely fashion, but there was someone running late for whom we had to wait: Weinstein.

After a short while, Weinstein boarded the plane with his wife, Georgina Chapman, two young children, and their nannies. He shook everybody's hand, said hello, and apologized for the delay. We could finally take off. As we taxied on the tarmac I tried to close my eyes and rest, but I couldn't—I had butterflies in my stomach and felt like I was on the brink of a major breakthrough in my life. I was on the plane that would take me to the place where I would meet the people who would help me in what by that point had become my life's mission.

During the flight we had quite a feast. There was unlimited food and free-flowing drinks. I must have eaten ten plates of food before I became too embarrassed to get more, so I deputized my fiancé to make multiple trips of his own to the buffet to bring me refills. The Gulfstream flew much faster than your average commercial plane, and the roaring sound of the engines hurt my ears. My fiancé casually asked our companions if they knew how much it cost to charter one of these Gulfstreams for the few hours it took to fly cross-country. They said it was over $100,000!

During 2016 I'd started to feel a bit of whiplash from my new life, and I really started to feel it now. I still remembered the prices my mother and I were sold for in China: $65 for her, less than $300 for me. I was flying through the same blue sky, lit by the same sun, looking down on the earth on which, only a few thousand miles away, we were sold into slavery, bought for sex. And now here I was, flying through the air for a price that could have purchased our freedom in an instant, along with that of hundreds if not thousands of other North Korean women and girls in China. And we were on our way to a conference where we were supposed to inspire each other to do amazing things with our lives! No private get-together is needed to figure out how to help people, no think tank or foundation or NGO—people with excess cash could, if they wanted, quite literally *buy* the freedom of their fellow human beings. But here we were, at a buffet moving 600 miles per hour at 30,000 feet in the air, lighting that cash on fire as we prepared to debate how to "do good" in the world.

Once we arrived in Santa Barbara, we checked into a beautiful five-star hotel called the Biltmore. Palm trees, cactuses, exotic desert plants, and an endless sea of flowers lined the resort, and the lobby smelled like eucalyptus and burning sage. The hotel room I was given was like a scene out of science fiction for me. Growing up in Hyesan, our faucet didn't have a warm water option; cold water came out of it only a handful of times in my life. Nor did we have in our home any space we might have called a "bathroom." We always washed our faces with the same water we used to wash any food we had, which was the same water we used to wash our rug and clean the floor. For all other matters, we just went outside. Throughout my whole childhood, I never slept on a softer or warmer surface than a cold cement floor. I remember seeing a cleaning woman pick up a room service tray from outside someone else's door, and thinking, *Americans could feed all of North Korea's starving children with nothing other than their trash.*

So it was with a kind of grim, guilt-inflected sense of excitement that I adjusted to my surroundings at this luxury hotel by the sea. That sense of tension was relieved a bit by the palpable, almost unbearable sense of anticipation in the air. In the next couple of days, I—little old Yeonmi from Hyesan—would speak to the world's movers and shakers, the ones who determine great events, people with real influence and power, which was what I needed access to if I was ever going to do good. And here they all were, amassed in one building on the Pacific Ocean, on the other side of which were the people I wanted to help. I was sure I would.

WARREN BUFFETT often suggests the following thought experiment: Assume that every human being currently alive, all eight billion souls on Earth, is a marble placed in a massive jar. If given the opportunity, would you put your marble in with the others, shake the jar, take another marble at random, and live that life instead? If the answer is no, then you know you have a blessed life.

For many years, I've lived with survivor's guilt, which the American Psychological Association defines as "remorse or guilt for having survived a catastrophic event when others did not." To this day, I have recurring dreams about the friends and family members I left behind in North Korea, and those who have suffered over the years since I became a sort of public figure, punished for their prior relationship with or proximity to me. After my mother and I defected, we used brokers in China and North Korea to send remittances back to family members. We learned in the years afterward that those brokers were no longer able to locate our relatives. It is likely they were imprisoned, disappeared, or killed.

The only way I've found that it's possible to stay sane is to try my best to derive meaning from my good fortune and what I've chosen to do with it. I know how blessed I am, and that my freedom wasn't earned. I'm not smarter or tougher than others who've fought for their freedom and come up short. In some moments, I see it as pure luck. In others, I feel that Someone above dealt me this hand, and expects me to do something with it beyond enjoying myself. He expects me not only to count my blessings but to share them.

In my better moments, therefore, I try to do everything in my power to remain grateful, to not grow bitter. I strive to continually remind myself, even when things are bleak, that there is hope for humanity, that justice *can* prevail, that good can and must be done, and that no one person or group of people is inherently evil—that there is evil in the world only because, like good, it runs through every human heart. Both good and evil run through small towns in North Korea; they run through farms in southern China; they run through shopping malls in Seoul and university campuses in New York. And so they must run through exclusive, luxury getaways for multimillionaires and billionaires, too, even if you have to squint to see it.

I tried hard to remember that in Santa Barbara. I had to.

ON THE first day of the conference, Harvey Weinstein gave a speech to everyone gathered there about his life: how he came from nothing, and how now, so improbably successful, he was giving back by helping disadvantaged people. I was deeply touched by his remarks. He is not from a wealthy family and had no connections to powerful people, but he did have grit and determination, and worked hard to become one of the most influential men in one of the most significant and culturally central industries in America, if not the world. As I listened to him speak, I thought his story was not all that dissimilar to my own; at least the context was. It was America that made his story possible, the land of opportunity where anyone who was willing to work hard and persevere could succeed, even a nobody from Flushing, Queens, the son of Polish immigrants; even a dirt-poor refugee from North Korea, who barely spoke English.

But then Weinstein went on to share a story about how he'd tricked a wealthy man from Saudi Arabia into giving money to one of his humanitarian causes: The Saudi businessman wanted to meet a famous actress, and Weinstein arranged for her to come to his hotel room, where the Saudi was waiting. Weinstein assured the audience that his wife was accompanying the actress, so everything was kosher.

On this sunny California morning in the fall of 2016, when Clinton's victory was all but assured and Weinstein was nothing but a genius who made the dreams of young actresses come true, everyone clapped and hooted passionately, and later that day enjoyed discussing their pleasant surprise at what a hero Weinstein was. I also thought very highly of him after his speech, but when I saw how the other Campfire attendees treated him at lunch—waiting in line to greet him, shaking his hand and embracing and kissing him reverentially—I started to think of him almost as a saint.

Less than a year later, he'd been credibly accused by eighty women of committing sexual crimes over the course of four decades. Some of those present at Campfire, including one very prominent actress, would become active and highly visible in the #MeToo movement, of which Weinstein was eventually the face. When I reached out to one of the people I'd met at Campfire and asked if she'd known about Weinstein's behavior before it became public, she said that of course she knew—everyone did. Did I not?

THE NEXT morning, it was my time to speak. I was preceded by virtual speeches from famous political figures, including Georgia representative John Lewis, who talked about the threat to American democracy posed by Trump's nomination, a theme that permeated Campfire, but on which I didn't plan to speak.

I took the stage and started by offering an apology to Jeff Bezos, who sat in the front row with his wife and young children. I tried to break the ice by explaining that the only reason I hadn't accepted his previous invitation was because I didn't know who he was, and that I still had no clue who almost anyone in the audience was, except for Tom Hanks and Reese Witherspoon. Everyone laughed, but a little more uncomfortably than I'd anticipated, as if I wasn't an immigrant from another country but a visitor from Saturn.

I then spoke about my journey from North Korea. By then I'd gathered that this was a less-than-serious gathering of the elites, where a greater number of delicious cocktails would be consumed than global problems solved, but I decided not to spare them any details. I described the starved and dead bodies I saw on the streets in Hyesan, and the risks my mother and I took to find a bowl of rice. I told them that one of the first things I witnessed after crossing the frozen Yalu River into China was the rape of my mother, that she was sold into sexual slavery, and that by the time we left China, I'd been raped by the broker who purchased me and suffered attempts by others, mostly human traffickers. I told this eminent audience about the hundreds of thousands of North Koreans still enslaved in China, many of them women and girls enduring the same treatment that my mother and I suffered.

It was evidently not the speech they were expecting. I could see looks of disbelief and sheer horror on the faces of many of those present. Jeff Bezos, for his part, looked to be in tears. After I was done speaking, and the audience ventured a unanimous but uncertain applause, Bezos raised his hand and asked a question that I still remember vividly.

"What kept you going against all the odds, and convinced you not to give up hope?"

Seeing his tears and those of others in the crowd, I struggled to choke back tears, too.

"My father," I replied. "My father told me that 'life is a gift and worth fighting for no matter what.' Even on his deathbed, he smiled at me and told me how precious life was, and asked me to never give up fighting for life. There are so many people in the world fighting for just one more day to live, and that's what my father did. He didn't take a second of life for granted, even though he was a fugitive, had no rights, and lived in excruciating pain from the cancer that was killing him.

"Since I was a child, he taught me that I had to be like a roly-poly toy. He said, 'Yeonmi-ya, no matter how much life pushes you down, you have to be resilient like the roly-poly doll, and always roll back up and fight again.'"

I relayed that my father's simple lesson was the only reason I was on the stage speaking to them that morning, because throughout my life, choosing to continue living has been the hardest choice of all.

After my speech, it finally happened: A few actors, businesspeople, and politicians came up to me and asked what I wanted them to ask—how they could help. I told them what it would cost to buy the freedom of an enslaved North Korean girl in China, but that China has a very sophisticated and impenetrable system of human trafficking, and so the single most effective thing they could do was to raise awareness about the Communist Party's sponsorship of the modern-day holocaust in North Korea, and about the modern-day slave trade of North Koreans in China.

The people who only a moment before had looked at me pleadingly for advice on how they could help people like my mother still stuck on the other side of the Pacific now looked at me again like I'd come from another galaxy, or else like a naive little girl who didn't understand the complexity or importance of China to their livelihoods. Their interest in me seemed to recede quickly, as did mine in Campfire.

IN EARLY 2017, one of the founders of Airbnb invited me to attend the Met Gala, an annual fundraising ball for the Metropolitan Museum of Art's fashion exhibit in New York City. The theme of that year's gala was something called "Edge," and they arranged for a stylist who brought dresses from museums in Australia. I had no idea what a big event it was and still didn't recognize most of the people in attendance. It was clearly a shallow and meaningless event, and my faith in gatherings like this had all but disappeared, but I figured that on the off chance I met one person who had the interest and wherewithal to take my advocacy at face value, it was worth a shot.

My hair, makeup, and nails were styled by different specialists several times in preparation for the evening. There was another specialist in charge of my dresses. For two days, there were four adults assigned to the task of making me up like an Asian porcelain doll, a look that made me uncomfortable in the extreme. When I expressed discomfort, I was told that was exactly the point: The theme was "Edge," and I had to feel "on it," because the purpose of the event that year was to help us "think outside the box." If Campfire revealed elites to be more immoral than I'd thought they were, the Met Gala revealed them to be dumber.

At the event itself I met people who seemed to pop out of my TV screen: Hugh Jackman, Kim Kardashian, Katy Perry, The Weeknd, Selena Gomez, the Jonas Brothers, and others who made me question whether I was in a fever dream as they walked and talked in front of me. During Katy Perry's performance, there was an incredibly tall man with his incredibly tall wife standing in front of me. I asked people at my table who these gigantic people were. They couldn't believe that I hadn't heard of Tom Brady and Gisele Bündchen. "He is a football player," they explained patiently to the visitor from Saturn. "He has won many Super Bowls." It was clear that this was something that I was meant to be impressed by, and I nodded in silent reverence.

The photographers who followed these celebrities everywhere screamed in a kind of possessed hysteria: "Please look over here, Selena!" and "Turn this way, Kim!" It reminded me of the Kim family's periodic trips to fake towns, fake factories, and fake stores, where they would pretend to inspect fake products, issue fake instructions, demonstrate fake satisfaction, and give a fake impromptu speech, where everyone present would feign applause or laughter or tears or whatever they felt was required of them in order to avoid being executed. Some sort of similar but entirely voluntary phenomenon seemed to be taking place at the Met Gala.

It would have all been amusing and funny if it weren't also a bit sad. I felt that night that the worst stereotypes of shallow and materialistic Western culture might actually contain a hint of truth. There seemed to be widespread, national interest in this cultlike event. My friends begged me to take pictures with celebrities and were reduced to tears with jealousy. They would literally cry when they received them.

For part of the evening I was seated next to Wendi Deng Murdoch, Rupert's ex-wife, and a few billionaires who owned some of the biggest tech companies in the world. They spoke of diamonds from Switzerland, and which supermodels were their favorites, and—brace yourself for shock—how much they hated Donald Trump. At one point in the evening, when I meekly ventured to share who I was and why on earth I'd been invited to attend this event with them, I was asked never to mention them in any of my speeches or in any public forum, due to their relationships with China.

Soon after I got up, I told the hosts I wouldn't be attending the afterparty—a concept that seemed so foreign to them that they had trouble deciphering my true intentions, and started explaining that the afterparty was where all the real fun would begin. But I couldn't wait to change out of the art-piece ball gown I was wearing, and had no interest in finding out what "real fun" for these people looked like. So I left.

OVER THE course of the following years, I delivered speeches at Google, Facebook, the United Nations, the U.S. Department of State, and the TED conference, describing what I knew to be happening under the Chinese Communist Party and the North Korean regime. It was the same sequence of events everywhere I went—lots of tears, lots of embracing and hand-shaking, lots of solicitous empathy and offers to help, all followed by lots of silence.

I later became aware that "Silence is violence" was a favorite political and cultural catchphrase of these elites, many of whom I saw again over the course of the next four years, this time on my TV—dressing in pink and marching against Trump, dressing in black and marching against police, dressing in green and marching against climate change, railing against the system that made them some of the most privileged human beings who've ever lived.

For the next four years, many of the people who appeared to listen intently as I told them what they could do to make a difference in the world instead spent their time warning the nation incessantly about fascists in the White House, of Russian puppets in the Oval Office, of white nationalists putting babies in cages. They advocated against truth in media and the neutral application of laws, which they no longer regarded as democratic norms but as unaffordable luxuries in the face of an existential threat: a president they didn't vote for.

Almost in unison, they started advocating for critical race theory and "antiracism," which more than anything else I'd encountered in

America reminded me of *Juche*, the North Korean version of Marxism-Leninism, with its arcane vocabulary and impenetrable set of ideas that pretend to serve political change but really just sort ordinary people into different identity categories that keep them as separate as possible from the elite. And like the elite in North Korea, the American elite used their new ideology to cancel and de-platform political and ideological dissidents.

It was a shocking four years for me as it was for millions of my fellow Americans, but there was one aspect of it that didn't surprise me, because I'd seen it up close on the conference circuit in 2016 and 2017: a certain brazen disingenuousness, which also reminded me of North Korea. In North Korea, it is not uncommon to see the well-fed son of a Party official lambast a farmer on the brink of starvation for insufficient loyalty to the Dear Leader. In post-2016 America, it started to become possible for a white magazine editor or white film producer or white tech CEO to lecture a Black construction worker or Latino small business owner who voted for Trump for his "self-hatred" or "internalized racism."

I started to wonder if that was the kind of thing they'd thought about me when I talked to them about my life and work. "Oh this poor little Asian girl, she's too stupid and naive to realize that the problem isn't dictatorship in North Korea or slavery in China. It's dictatorship and slavery in America!"

ALLOW ME one final anecdote, which is notable because it was the first time I witnessed blatant corruption in America.

One day, I received an invitation to another one of these "off-the-record" private dinners, this time hosted by Tina Brown, of Women in the World and the *Daily Beast*. It was an intimate evening that Tina cohosted with Brian Moynihan, the CEO of Bank of America, in late September of 2019 at the five-star St. Regis Hotel in New York during the United Nations General Assembly. Other invitees included Imran Khan, the prime minister of Pakistan, and Speaker of the House Nancy Pelosi. There were also several tycoons from media, fashion, Hollywood, tech, finance, and academia. I remember one *New York Times* journalist seated next to a famous Chinese venture capitalist.

During the cocktail hour, I approached Speaker Pelosi and introduced myself as a North Korean defector and survivor of sexual slavery in China who was now fighting for the international community's support for people like me. She gave a very diplomatic response and casually brushed me off. She clearly had something else on her mind.

Later that evening, she gave remarks to the rest of the invitees, who, remember, included not only many investors but also foreign heads of state. She told us all that the next day, on September 24, she was going to announce a formal impeachment inquiry of President Trump, and that the news would go out that morning. "You all know what this means," she said. "You need to prepare."

The message was clear to me: When the impeachment news comes out, the market will fall. You have one night only to short it. The next day, like clockwork, the *Washington Post* announced the impeachment inquiry, and the market fell.

A few weeks later, Pelosi said in an interview with *Politico*, "If we allow one president—any president, no matter who she or he may be—to go down this path, we are saying goodbye to the republic and hello to a president-king."

PART II

ON THE ROAD TO RUIN

5

Values in Decline

What I love most about the United States of America, both in theory and in practice, is its commitment to each individual's unalienable rights to life, liberty, and *the pursuit of happiness*. It's difficult to communicate to Americans who were born here just how unusual that last right is as a value, let alone a value held by the state. Most countries are committed to either abstract ideas like the "glory" or "majesty" or "destiny" of a people or government, or to something ruthlessly practical, like its own security or survival. But America is dedicated to the right of each inhabitant to try his or her best to be *happy*. This of course does not guarantee that anyone in particular will actually *be* happy. But America is founded on the idea that no person or group of people or institution should be allowed to obstruct anyone else's freedom to *attempt* to be happy. The document that enshrines this idea—the Declaration of Independence—is written in sublime language to match this utterly sublime idea, and makes me proud not only to be American but to be human.

But the right to pursue happiness, like self-government and democracy itself, does come with certain obligations. It is a difficult right to sustain unless the people themselves are committed to civic duty, individual responsibility, hard work, and a certain degree of personal virtue. The Jeffersonian image of "the right to pursue happiness" is not of the Wolf of Wall Street, leaving trails of lies, drug abuse, broken relationships, and professional and familial wreckage. It is about starting your own business, owning your own property, raising your own family, and participating in your own community in whatever way you see fit, within the bounds of the law and respect for the rights of others.

As I approached my midtwenties, it became harder and harder not to notice what the "right to pursue happiness" meant for many Americans of my generation. New York City in particular seemed to encourage and elevate the boundless pursuit of cardinal sins as a virtue in itself: the oozing vanity of the fashion and nightlife industries, the insatiable greed of the financial world, the envy of power and material gain that seemed to make everyone I knew almost hopelessly jealous of others and therefore unhappy with their own lives.

And then there was lust.

Many of my girlfriends in New York were in the habit of voluntarily pursuing one-night stands on many weekends, which only seemed to subject them to a broader sense of regret and loneliness. When one of them showed me her mobile dating app, which at that point was a concept I'd never heard of, I thought it was a joke—that all the men on there must be fake. Some of my older friends in particular, including married ones, encouraged me to spend these years, my early twenties, dating around without commitment. They were particularly fond of aquatic metaphors like "test the waters," "dip your toe," and "there are so many fish in the sea," which I had and still have trouble grasping.

Still, for a time I was amused by the novelty of it all. The freedom to love whomever you want was and remains a powerful idea for me. In North Korea, the strict caste system called *songbun* prohibits intermarriage or even friendly association between different classes, which is in part designed to prevent upward mobility. If a member of a lower caste does marry someone from a higher caste, the member of the higher caste gets demoted to the lower—never the reverse. This of course disincentivizes people from mixing and "marrying down." Such is the classless paradise of socialism: Most marriages in North Korea are arranged between families or else assigned by the government. The concept of dating has slowly penetrated the younger strata of society, as more young people have been exposed to smuggled South Korean television dramas. But when it comes to marriage, the young remain wary of ever doing anything that might bring down their family's status.

Surprisingly, things weren't altogether different in that sense when I moved to South Korea, where I was heavily discriminated against because of my origin and my difficulties keeping up with the academic rat race. Even though it's democratic, capitalist, and broadly aligned with the United States and the West, South Korea remains a very homogeneous society in which people from poor countries like North Korea and other underdeveloped Southeast Asian countries are looked down upon. To this day, my mother gets mocked by street vendors and her own neighbors in South Korea for her northern accent.

In America, however, even though I spoke badly broken English with a heavy East Asian accent, no one seemed to care. I was welcomed with open arms, and felt truly accepted for the first time in my life. People were open-minded and compassionate, and I was filled with joy to find that Dr. King's dream was a reality—that nearly all Americans seemed ready to judge me not by the color of my skin, but by the content of my character. That made the prospect of meeting a romantic companion exciting, If everyone here had the freedom to date whoever they wanted without prejudice, and New York was a racial, ethnic, and religious melting pot, then it would be as if I had the whole world at my fingertips—not only would I not be restricted to dating and eventually marrying a man from Korea and from my own low caste, but I would have the chance to truly fall in love. Indeed, my first relationship in America was with a Jewish guy whose family escaped the Soviet Union when he was eight years old—our different ethnicities, religions, and backgrounds proved no obstacle.

SOME OF my girlfriends were less lucky. I couldn't help but notice that in the large metropolises of New York, Los Angeles, and San Francisco in particular, they struggled to find partners who were serious and willing to commit to them. I have to admit, I was a bit shocked by this. With all the deep flaws of North Korean men and their sometimes primitive attitudes toward women, dating is one thing they take seriously and for which they're willing to act responsibly. Cosmopolitan men, apparently, not so much.

Most men I met in New York City in particular were a bit of a mystery to me. In North Korea, "dating material" and "marriage material" are not relevant categories (or categories that even exist). People date in order to marry, and they marry in order to raise a family. Dating can be an exciting experience, but it's still a relatively solemn and dignified process. In New York, however, people seemed to date mostly to get drunk and have sex. My girlfriends sometimes called or texted me on Sunday morning to share their disappointment that the guy they got drunk and had sex with on the previous Friday had gone silent, or even that their boyfriends of some substantial period of time decided to break things off once the issue of engagement or even just exclusivity was raised.

In North Korea, a man's primary responsibility to women is to protect and provide for them. Perhaps that is far too narrow and suffocating of a gender dynamic, but I started to realize that I at least preferred it to the modern Western dynamic in which men are apparently encouraged to feel no responsibility whatsoever for the women they court.

Keep in mind that many of my girlfriends in New York at this point were still my fellow students from Columbia, where we were taught (and many of them evidently believed in) "post-feminism": the idea that gender itself is nothing more than an ideological construct invented by men to oppress women. (If you noticed a blaring contradiction in that definition, you're not alone.) This often caused them to live lives of almost comical hypocrisy: "There is no difference between men and women, marriage is antiquated, and children are a burden. Why don't any of these men want to be exclusive with me or even just call me back?"

It seemed painfully obvious to me that if men really had invented an ideological construct that served no purpose other than to give them everything they wanted, "post-feminism" was clearly it! Twice the sex, none of the responsibility. No wonder the men I knew in New York typically seemed much happier than my ultra-woke girlfriends. Even some of the men I knew in their fifties still dated young women in their twenties, and often in "open" relationships. The women I knew in their thirties and early forties seemed to hate women my age with a passionate intensity, presumably because they suddenly realized they were running out of time and were miserable. Most of them seemed to go to therapy every week, and would talk about their therapist the way they would talk about their dates—how hard it was to find a good one, how they could never do without therapy but also felt like they weren't making progress.

In the midst of arguing that gender is a construct, complaining about "toxic masculinity" and "mansplaining," declaring that the idea of a "protector" or "provider" is sexist, that marriage is outdated, and that children rob you of your freedom, no one seemed to stop and wonder if they might be personally responsible for their own unhappiness.

From then on, whenever a man I was interested in asked me out on a date, I told him that I only dated exclusively, and only with the intention of eventually getting married. My girlfriends of course advised me not to say such things, which would scare the wits out of any sane young man and send him running in the opposite direction. But I just figured that any man who would be frightened of commitment would probably also be too frightened to be responsible or loving, and therefore not worth my time. In any case, I wasn't afraid of being single, which to me was infinitely better than being with the wrong person, or being in a relationship for the wrong reasons.

Thankfully, my first boyfriend was a gentleman. He was honest and very responsible. It was also the first time I'd ever become romantic with anyone. It was hard at first, but I was happy to have found someone who shared many of my values. I was twenty-one and still relatively new in America, and unsure of myself and my new surroundings, and eventually succumbed to peer pressure. After a year of dating, I broke up with him, feeling I was doing something wrong by not "testing the waters" and meeting the "other fish in the sea." But I immediately realized that this kind of thing didn't make me happy at all.

THEN IN the hot and humid summer of 2016, at a friend's birthday party, I met a very unusual "American Bastard." He knew quite a bit about North Korea, which he'd taken an interest in and read books and watched documentaries about, and seemed to genuinely care about the suffering of people there. He also shared my own values about the importance of family. We fell in love very quickly, and in late 2016, when he was thirty-two and I was twenty-three, we got married in downtown Manhattan. From the venue where we held the ceremony, you could see the Statue of Liberty in the distance. Only in America, I remember thinking that day, would my story be possible.

In North Korea, international marriages are illegal. Multiracial babies are often killed and pregnant women are forced into getting abortions if the unborn child is not a "pureblood." Women who defect to China only to be raped sometimes get pregnant. If caught and sent back to North Korea, the authorities use brutal methods to forcibly abort the pregnancy. They will inject pregnant women with saltwater syringes, kick their stomachs repeatedly, or place a long wooden board on their belly and force young kids to jump on it. If, by some miracle, the child is born anyway, the regime will sometimes seal the innocent baby in a box and leave it to die.

How impossibly far I'd come from that nightmare: marrying an American man on the island of Manhattan in full view of Lady Liberty.

How I loved every moment of my new life, every inch of this new country, flaws and all, and how truly grateful I was for the freedom to go wherever my heart led me.

The strongest bond that my husband and I shared was our common longing for meaning and to live rewarding lives. I knew well how challenging life could be when bereft of meaning. As Viktor E. Frankl, the Holocaust survivor and great psychiatrist, notes in his masterpiece, *Man's Search for Meaning,* "If you find a why, then you can bear any how." My husband and I were committed to the "why," which included first and foremost having a family.

Soon after our marriage, we tried to have a baby. I was, however, and still am, extremely underweight, due to the first fourteen year of my life, when I was severely malnourished. I'm five feet two inches tall, but even in 2016, I weighed less than eighty pounds. We eventually realized that the malnutrition and trauma of my childhood and growing up would make a natural pregnancy impossible for me. So we decided to pursue in vitro fertilization (IVF). How astonishing, I remember thinking, that I now had the option of accessing this extraordinary technology in order to fulfill my dream of becoming a mother, while my hometown of Hyesan doesn't even have reliable electricity.

Early on countless mornings, I went to the infertility clinic to have my blood drawn and check if I was pregnant. I remember seeing so many clearly very bright and ambitious women there, who were as desperate as I was to become pregnant. As sad as it was to find so many women having such a hard time, it was inspiring, really, to see all these accomplished and powerful women trying so hard to become mothers. After several injections and trials, and after the third time of trying IVF, in the summer of 2017, I finally got pregnant.

The day I found out was one of the happiest of my life. When I got the results of the test, in fact, I was on my way to the New York Gay Pride Parade with my sister-in-law. The strongest emotion I remember that day was one of deep, deep gratitude for the miraculous process that had begun inside of me.

During the pregnancy I got regular sonograms, and my doctor advised me to take prenatal vitamins and iron supplements. I remember thinking then that all the suffering I'd endured in life up until that point had been worth it, because it meant that my child was going to have a wonderful life here in America, starting even with the vitamins I'd be able to provide them while still in the womb.

You can imagine, then, what I thought by this point of the constant and increasingly shrill stream of news, debates, and conversations about the fascist hellhole that America had become.

I TOOK a semester off from Columbia and moved with my husband to Chicago, where his company was located, to give birth to a son. It was early in 2018, and like many other American mothers, I was quite overwhelmed to discover all the things you're expected to buy, have, and know in order to care for an American baby! I didn't know a thing about strollers, formula, bottles, bottle warmers, bottle sterilizers, swings, cribs, bathtubs, disposable diapers, non-disposable diapers, wipes, pumps, or bibs, let alone concepts like "sleep training" and "self-led weaning."

Needless to say, hardly any of this exists in North Korea. If a North Korean mother can't produce breast milk, and there's no wet nurse around, the baby will die of starvation. This is often the case, because severe and widespread malnutrition means many North Korean women cannot lactate. A far cry from raising children in America, where parents buy products like the "Frida," which allows you to suck the snot out of your baby's nose, and the "Windi," which helps ease their gas.

Now in the great Midwest, every day I spent in the United States made me more and more grateful for the Americans who came before me and built this just and prosperous land. As overwhelming as it was to prepare for childbirth, I couldn't help but admire the wonders of the free market and the entrepreneurialism that went into the medical care, child care, and parenting products that American parents were expected to take advantage of, and to which even Americans of limited means still had some modicum of access.

I also couldn't help but think of my father. If he only knew what my later life would be like, what possibilities for safety and prosperity and freedom awaited me and my son, his grandchild, that would have been enough for him.

I was often too drunk with the joys of pregnancy and the awe of becoming an American mother to pay much attention to the strange questions my nurses and doctor would ask during each checkup. "Do you feel depressed?" "Do you feel safe at home?" And then, postpartum, "Are you having suicidal thoughts?" Mobile apps I was advised to download also kept tabs on my inner life, warning me of the challenges ahead, how my body would change in ways that would make me depressed, the mood swings I'd feel, reminding me that it was okay and normal to "feel sad" about having a baby, and ways to seek professional help to deal with it.

Pregnancy is certainly challenging, postpartum depression is indeed very real for many women, and I don't minimize the burdensome sacrifices that mothers and expecting mothers are called upon to make. But all of this struck me as utterly bizarre. Even in a country like North Korea, which places as little value on human life as it's possible to do, pregnancy and childbirth are still considered by the people who go through it (as opposed to the state) as sacred and precious. It is inconceivable for a North Korean woman to weigh a cost-benefit analysis for having a child the way many American women are encouraged to do: "On the one hand, I will create a human life and love it and be loved by it like nothing else in the world. On the other hand, I'll gain weight and become temporarily less attractive to men who aren't my husband. Is this really worth it?"

Yes, dear reader. It is.

THE DAY my son was born was the happiest day of my life. In those early moments, and to this day, there was nothing else in the world that mattered to me.

On the day of the delivery, I underwent a cesarean section because my body wasn't big enough to allow for a safe natural birth. When the doctors pulled him out of my belly and placed him on my chest where I could hold him in my arms and touch his skin with my cheeks, I couldn't believe how lucky I was to be his mother. I simply couldn't believe that someone like me could possibly deserve to be the mother to such a wonderful little boy like him. I remember thinking then of my ancestors, the ones from way, way back, and imagined all the women who fought through wilderness and drought and famine and war to give birth, to continue life, so that one day I could do so in a hospital, in peace and in health.

It was then that I realized what happiness is. It's nothing other than a synonym for love and gratitude. Happiness is not material success or recognition or even comfort. It's becoming a parent, being a good daughter, being a good friend, and lending a helping hand to anyone less fortunate. What this meant was that finding meaning in life was not an arduous search that may or may not end in gratification. Meaning, it turns out, is not difficult to find at all. As many wise people have pointed out, happiness is a choice. My mother once told me that without gratitude, happiness is impossible. "When I ask God for happiness," she said, "he tells me instead to learn to be grateful." She (and He) was right.

Despite the indescribable horrors she's been through in life, my mother is to this day the happiest person I know. She has been a sex slave, a rape victim, an inmate, forcibly separated from her children and husband, and a refugee. And yet she is genuinely, authentically grateful and happy, and almost always has been. I'd never quite understood it. But now, I felt, I did.

6

Victimhood and Oppression

I was absolutely determined to raise my son to be resilient, to be grateful, and to be happy—all the qualities I felt were painfully absent in many of the Americans my age I'd met during my years as a college student. I would have wanted to raise him that way in any case, but I also knew the social and professional world into which he was being born.

In many ways, my son is among the luckiest human beings who've ever existed—he was born in the United States of America in the twenty-first century. In another sense, though, he's totally screwed. He is half Caucasian, half Asian—the very peak of the "privilege" pyramid. Regardless of his actual family background, no one will ever be impressed by his achievements; no one will feel sorry for his failures. His successes will be attributed to factors outside of his own control; his mistakes won't be easily forgiven. He will be seen as an oppressor, or as an exploiter and beneficiary of the oppression of others, even if he's a kind and decent and respectful boy and man. It won't matter that his mother was a refugee from a dictatorship, that the women in his family were sold into slavery, or that his life itself is a kind of improbable miracle. I know for a fact that he'll have to fight for respect.

And so I knew from day one that my son would have to be a fighter. And there's only one way to become one.

I WAS thirteen years old when my parents and I lost track of my older sister, Eunmi, who was sixteen at the time. We didn't have any food in the house and all feared the very real and imminent possibility of starvation. It was March 26, 2007, and my sister escaped Hyesan to China via the Yalu River. She had left me a note, instructing me to come to China and find her.

Our journey toward reunification was ridden with turmoil and painful trials. After the unspeakable terrors of the Chinese sex trade, I finally saw my sister again in Seoul, South Korea, when I was twenty years old after South Korean intelligence had put us in touch with each other. We were no longer teenagers or young women; seven whole years had passed, an eternity for girls that age.

Early on in my life in South Korea, the one insight that helped me get through whatever trauma I continued to experience and to live life with gratitude and optimism was that there is no end to self-pity. Like a bottomless well or an infinite tunnel, no matter how deep you go into self-pity, no matter how much you think you're benefiting from it or justified in plumbing its depths, there is simply no end. Take the plunge, and you will struggle to ever find your way back out.

We live in a physical world, and our bodies are part of that world; as such, almost everything we experience takes place within the confines of our brain. It is our brain that is in charge of our relation to the external world, and that interprets the world and our experiences in it. Thankfully, the brain does not have "a life of its own"—it is actually one of the most controllable organs in our bodies, as long as we're aware of it. If suffering is experienced in the brain only (as opposed to physical forms of suffering, like torture or disease), then by definition, that suffering is a *decision*. That's why I strongly believe that the great majority of the suffering we experience is actually caused by ourselves and the decisions we make (or don't make). In other words, feelings of devastation mostly come from the way we *think* about "the problem," rarely from the problem itself.

Partly because of what I learned from my parents and partly because of my natural wiring, I felt these things in my bones from a fairly early age, even before I had the wherewithal to articulate them, and so I told my sister early and often not to get into the habit of thinking of herself as "poor me." Even when we were on our own without our parents and there was no food to eat, the mere fact that we were living and breathing meant that we had more to be grateful for than not. When we were reunited in Seoul all those years later, I reminded my sister that unlike us, there were countless North Koreans who still wished for a better life, fought for a better life, but ultimately didn't make it out. It was an insight and attitude that came less naturally to Eunmi than it did to me. I felt frustrated, but I understood.

I also know that trauma is a real phenomenon. The difficulties experienced by survivors of wars, famines, familial abuse, and sexual violence are evidence that trauma is a deep and common problem for millions of people. I, too, sometimes feel triggered; I often feel frightened or cornered into irrational thoughts that have nothing to do with the present and everything to do with the past. On some nights, I still wake up from nightmares covered in sweat. On others—less frequently now, but the problem still persists—I wake up screaming. When it happens, instead of despairing over my condition, I try to focus on how lucky I am that when I wake up from my nightmares, my reality is infinitely better: safe and comfortable, with everything I need.

Many Americans and other people around the world have asked me how it's possible, as I wrote in my first book, that I'm actually grateful to have been born in North Korea. I understand their confusion. I typically reply that if I hadn't experienced hunger, injustice, oppression, and the loss of loved ones, I wouldn't be able to appreciate the prosperity, justice, safety, and freedom that I experience with such passionate intensity every day in America. It's all, of course, about perspective—and because I was born in North Korea, I have more of it than most. And that's helped me be a fighter.

I want my son to have the same perspective, but don't want him to have to endure the trauma that I went through to obtain it. So I try to instill it in him by setting a good example, and by teaching him, like my father and mother taught me.

But as every parent knows, as you send your children out into society—even one as admirable, just, and free as America's—it's hard not to worry about the examples they'll absorb and the teachers they'll meet out there in the world. And for my son, I worry.

THE CANADIAN psychologist and author Jordan Peterson is fond of pointing out that "suffering is an integral part of existence." All the world's major religions, whether Abrahamic or Eastern, polytheistic or monotheistic, agree that suffering is essential to human life, including to the good life. Buddhism in particular has this concept at its core, outlined by the Four Noble Truths:

> The First is that *life is suffering*.
> The Second is that *the cause of suffering is desire*.
> The Third is that *the end of suffering is caused by the end of desire*.
> The Fourth is that *suffering and desire can be overcome through the Noble Eightfold Path*.

But *why* is life intertwined with suffering? This is the question that preoccupies the Abrahamic religions in particular, which Peterson often cites to propose three possible answers. First, the core reason behind human suffering is that *we are all deemed insufficient in the eyes of society*. But because a society's value system is often pretty arbitrary, it could be argued that we as individuals are not in fact insufficient, but rather that society itself is judgmental and often tyrannical, and should be modified to reduce its authoritarian tendencies.

The second reason for suffering is that, compared with nature and the scale of the universe, humans are fragile beings with tiny life spans who must experience the death and demise of our loved ones, and endure the inevitable sense of loss, loneliness, and insignificance that comes with it.

That much makes sense. But it's not the whole picture. The third and biggest element in human suffering is actually *unnecessary suffering*—the type that is within our control to stop and that is our own doing in the first place. We know perfectly well when we are being lazy, or irresponsible, or greedy, or making foolish choices. The Lebanese American writer Khalil Gibran described this phenomenon beautifully in his poetic and almost biblical book *The Prophet*:

You are good when you are one with yourself.
Yet when you are not one with yourself you are not evil.
For a divided house is not a den of thieves; it is only a divided house.
And a ship without rudder may wander aimlessly among perilous
  isles yet sink not to the bottom.

A ship without a rudder. How many of us go through life feeling this way? That we are aimlessly sailing through the waves and currents of life, thrown uncontrollably from one side to another? Whether you can take solace in ancient wisdom like the Buddha's, or modern poets like Gibran, or contemporary thinkers like Peterson, the answer is the same: A certain degree of suffering is natural, even essential, to human life—but the only way through, the only path for righting the ship, is to be completely, entirely at one with yourself: to be authentically you. Until then, it's impossible to achieve the responsibility and find the meaning required to do away with unnecessary suffering.

Even in his first five years of life, I've tried to instill this wisdom in my son, because I know he probably won't receive it in schools, which increasingly across America have stopped teaching students that suffering is either necessary or within their power to control. More and more, the institutions that educate and help us raise our children teach them that all suffering comes from the first factor alone: social oppression, in the form of American capitalist democracy.

AS I alluded to in the introduction, for the duration of my time in the United States, I've been the target of attacks and accusations of being "right wing" or "far right," almost exclusively for what I've said in public about the Chinese and North Korean regimes—both of which the U.S. government itself, under different administrations, has labeled enemies or competitors. But such attempts at cancellation have also been motivated by my criticisms of elements of America's own political culture, which remind me of the totalitarian tendencies I know so well from my early life. The attacks and accusations are never totally monolithic, but they do tend to come from one political camp in particular: Americans who consider themselves Marxist, Leninist, Maoist, Communist, Socialist, Democratic Socialist, or more broadly, of "the Left."

I've noticed that these fellow Americans of mine seem to work mostly in schools, universities, media, large corporations, NGOs, foundations, activist organizations, and government bureaucracies. They tend not to be first-generation immigrants, but people who were born in America, and thus people who have never actually lived under the kind of political and social system they believe to be superior to America's capitalist democracy.

It is, of course, their right to believe in and advocate for whatever kind of nonsense suits them—that's what democracy is. But the reason it concerns me is because the same people who have accused me of being outside the boundaries of acceptable political discourse for criticizing communism tend to also be the people who are most visible and influential in the world my young son is entering. They staff the institutions responsible for his education; they create the information environment that is meant to curate his understanding of the outside world; they are charged with providing many of the social services on which he and his community rely. And they are committed to supporting an ideology that bears a close resemblance to the one from which I barely escaped: leftism.

It's important to distinguish leftism from liberalism. Liberalism has its foundation in liberty and individual rights: freedom of speech, of the press, of religion, and of the market. Leftism has its foundation in the centralization of these rights not in the individual but in groups organized and directed by the state. Liberalism values color blindness—that the color of one's skin determines and should determine nothing. Leftists believe that almost everything in society can and should be determined by race alone. Liberalism promotes racial integration and inclusivity; leftism promotes increased racial segregation and exclusion.

Leftists and liberals differ on their attitude toward capitalism, too. For liberals, capitalism is the only proven method of bringing the greatest number of people possible out of poverty. For leftists, capitalism is the cause of, rather than the solution to, poverty, and must be extinguished through the elimination of free markets and the greater centralization of state power over the economy and individual decision-making. As for nationalism and patriotism, liberals believe in the necessity of nation-states that have borders, citizenship, and sovereignty, while leftists believe only in open borders and that all human beings should be "citizens of the world." (I'd like to invite leftists to experience their world citizenship from the comfort of North Korea—enjoy!) Thus, while liberals often acknowledge America's flaws and imperfections, they nonetheless believe that the United States is deserving of love, devotion, and respect. Leftists, on the other hand, believe America is uniquely racist, sexist, homophobic, xenophobic, and imperialist.

Again, all Americans are entitled to their own foolishness. But the problem is that the Left has done a thorough job of conflating itself with liberalism in the minds of the public, collapsing America's once-great and necessary left flank—which used to be devoted to real economic solidarity and racial equality—into an oligarchic ideology of economic exploitation and racial division. The conflation of leftism with liberalism is what allows many American leftists to advocate for the superiority of an authoritarian social and political system without ever having to actually live under or suffer the consequences of it. They therefore continue to enjoy the fruits of democratic capitalism—wealth, social mobility, freedom of speech and association, property ownership—while advocating for its destruction.

This tends to lead to a kind of cognitive dissonance and self-hatred that expresses itself in increasingly shrill in-group competition about who suffers more under the current system. For someone like New York representative Alexandria Ocasio-Cortez, for example, the more personal success she accumulates—the more profitably she uses American democratic capitalism to achieve her personal, professional, reputational, and financial ambitions—the more she feels obligated to perform her own imagined victimization, her own uncontrollable suffering, and her own supposed opposition to the very system she so effectively utilizes.

The fact that leftists tend to benefit so greatly from American democratic capitalism while rhetorically advocating for its destruction also helps explain why they are so much less focused on the future than on the past. Stuck in their own self-made contradictions about current American life, from which they profit so handsomely, leftists tend to focus on the unalterable past as a way of perpetuating their own perceived victimhood and punishing their ideological opponents. Hence, a distant descendant of nineteenth-century African slaves who works at Goldman Sachs or studies at Harvard is a victim. The first-generation immigrant child of a twenty-first-century Chinese slave who goes to public school is not.

I write all this by way of trying to explain the kind of ideology to which I worry about subjecting my son. If many or most teachers and educators see it as their duty, or even just their professional obligation, to teach students that all of human history is just a catalog of oppression, and that the United States exists only to oppress them, what are our children's prospects for living joyful and meaningful lives? How will they see their own capacities for taking control of their lives? How will they see their own prospects for overcoming life's many challenges, and for making changes to improve themselves as individuals and members of their communities?

THE FOUNDING despot of North Korea, Kim Il Sung, rose to power on the premise not only of being a great leader, but of being a god. He did so in part by promising to solve all forms of inequality and injustice, which he explained were simple and unnecessary problems that required simple, obvious solutions. The root cause of both inequality and injustice, he explained, was a capitalist conspiracy to make everyone pay money for essential services that they should be getting for free: education, health care, housing, food—*everything* people need to survive and thrive. And in order to make these services and resources free and accessible to everyone, all forms of private ownership had to be abolished: "Capitalists" (which is to say, ordinary citizens) were henceforth no longer allowed to own their own schools, or hospitals, or houses, or farms. The state (which is to say, those with military and police power) confiscated them. Needless to say, the results were catastrophic—just as they were in China, Vietnam, Cuba, the Soviet Union, Yugoslavia, and the Warsaw Pact countries.

There is much one can say about the shortcomings of education, health care, housing, and food security in America, and about the dire need to reform and improve them. But the leftist insistence on nationalizing these services and resources in order to make them free—as if the various failings in these sectors can be attributed to the mere existence and legality of private ownership—contains dangerous echoes of the North Korean model. Again, to believe that the answers to social problems lie not in innovation, creativity, and a certain measure of personal and communal responsibility, but rather in the centralization of state power and the eradication of private ownership, is just a variation on the leftist theme of victimhood and oppression, which really only serves to mask the emergence and power of an oligarchy.

I experienced the consequences of this process firsthand in North Korea. When the regime abolished private ownership and stole everything the people had, the result, of course, was not free and open access to the services and resources on which ordinary people depend—it was the simple theft of those resources by the supporters and enforcers of the regime. This process didn't just enrich the regime itself, it created an elite class of mid-level officials, bureaucrats, managers, and military officers who very much enjoy the spoils of wealth, property, and inequality, while continuing to advocate for socialist revolution. (I hope this is starting to sound familiar.)

To keep the painfully obvious contradictions in this system from bursting out into the open, the regime and its bloodhounds—the elite overclass—made use of land ownership the way today's leftist elite in America makes use of race. In North Korea, if your ancestors were peasants, then your blood—literally, your very *genes*—are considered noble, because it's uncontaminated by the blood of a land-owning, capitalist oppressor. By the same token, if your ancestors did own land, that means that the blood of an oppressor flows within you—and you're forever tainted.

This utter nonsense about genetic complicity in what the regime considers to be capitalist crimes allows it to divide the people arbitrarily between oppressors and oppressed, which determines who is deserving of education, who of medical care, who of housing, and who of food (which simply masks the reality that there is not enough of any of these things to go around). Conveniently enough, every member of the ruling elite in North Korea happens to have untainted blood; every prisoner, laborer, slave, and victim of starvation happens to have the blood of an oppressor.

Funny how that works.

IN THE last few years, I've taken a particular interest in attempts to divide Americans into oppressors and oppressed because I've found myself—and my son will find himself—on a side of the divide I didn't exactly expect.

I've never felt like a victim, and I've certainly never wanted anyone in America or anywhere else to treat me like one. But if you'd told me that the United States is a country in which some people are considered victims based on the color of their skin, while some are considered oppressors based on the color of theirs, I would have assumed that Asian Americans might fall into the former camp, for obvious historical reasons.

In the mid-to-late nineteenth century, thousands of manual laborers from China were brought over to build the transcontinental railroad. They were paid below-subsistence wages and made to sleep outside in tents, while white American workers received higher pay and slept in train cars. At the turn of the twentieth century, the United States enacted anti-Asian immigration policies to combat what was then known as the "yellow peril," an existential fear that "hordes" of yellow Asian people, who were often depicted in newspapers as primates and children, would infect white, Christian America. As Americans colonized the Philippines through the 1930s, Filipinos became known as a "contaminated race." During World War II, Japanese Americans—that is, U.S. citizens of Japanese descent—were arrested and incarcerated in isolated internment camps, on suspicion of aiding the country's fascist enemy. During the later Cold War, unwelcome refugees from the communist dictatorship in Vietnam—where America played a large role in much of the wartime suffering and misery—were derisively known as "boat people."

The history of Asian Americans is complex and multifaceted, but for most of American history, this community suffered from state-sanctioned racism, exploitation, segregation, and unspeakable civil rights violations. So does that mean that today's descendants of the first several waves of Asian immigration are considered to have the "blood" of the oppressed?

Quite the contrary. As of the summer of 2022, the U.S. Supreme Court has agreed to hear a case brought by Asian-American college students alleging well-founded and well-documented suspicions of discrimination at Harvard and other elite universities, including the use of informal quota systems, much like the Ivy League maintained Jewish quotas in the early twentieth century. Over the past decade, in fact, the share of Asian-American students at Harvard has remained constant at 20 percent, despite the community's position as the fastest-growing group in the United States. Estimates by an economist hired by the plaintiffs in the Supreme Court case found that "a male non-poor Asian-American applicant with the qualifications to have a 25% chance of admission to Harvard would have a 36% chance if he were white. If he were Hispanic, that would be 77%; if Black, it would rise to 95%."

The need to put a cap on Asian American academic achievement comes from their disproportionate performance success in standardized testing—which of course is not the result of their "blood," but of whatever claims the families and communities have to hard work, study, and academic rigor. But the attempt to paint their academic success as somehow related to the color of their skin is supported by popular leftist ideologues such as Boston University professor Ibram X. Kendi, of "antiracism" fame. In 2020, during the furor over Asian American quotas in elite universities, Kendi claimed, "Standardized tests have become the most effective racist weapon ever devised to objectively degrade Black and Brown minds and legally exclude their bodies from prestigious schools."

Asians benefit from standardized tests, standardized tests are weapons of racism, therefore, Asians are racist oppressors. Get it?

Or take the dramatic surge in violent attacks against Asian Americans that began after the summer of 2020. These innocent victims of random, unjustified beatings by strangers on the street had (and have) only one hope of eliciting any kind of sympathy, outrage, or even just attention from leftist elites: if their attackers were white (the very pinnacle of racist oppressor). Kendi and other activists tried hard to paint the wave of attacks as an example of "white supremacy," but according to national crime data that includes "Asian American" as a category of crime victim, this isn't true. Among the Asian Americans who suffered from violent attacks starting in 2020, 27.5 percent of their attackers were Black, 24.1 percent were white,

21.4 percent were Latino and "other" combined, and 24.1 percent were Asian.

This helps explain why hardly anyone in the media or leftist politics, who are otherwise so preoccupied with covering race-based violence, even deigned to cover the wave of attacks on Asian Americans. The fact that a plurality of the criminal perpetrators had "oppressed blood," and that the victims all had "oppressor blood," put this national outrage beyond the boundaries of acceptable discourse. (The fact that Asian Americans, broadly defined, vote for the Democratic Party by a margin of two to one earns them no brownie points with the leftist elite.)

Besides performing too well on standardized tests and being targeted for violent attacks by members of the wrong ethnic groups, today's Asian Americans have committed the additional and especially unforgivable infraction of being too happy and patriotic. In one poll or survey after another, Asian Americans report being predominantly satisfied with their quality of life, optimistic about the future, and proud of their country. (The only statistic that goes in the other direction is the increasing number of Asian Americans who say they fear for their physical safety as a result of discrimination.) But it doesn't necessarily take a poll to figure that out: Asian immigrants overtook Hispanic immigrants as the fastest-growing immigrant group in America over a decade ago, and the majority of those who come to America do so with the intention of staying and becoming citizens.

Economists call this "revealed preference"—that people's true beliefs (as opposed to the ones they merely *claim* to have) can be understood in how they choose to spend their money and where they choose to live. This is also sometimes called "voting with your feet"—people who truly *are* oppressed (rather than just claim to *feel* oppressed) tend to move somewhere else where they are freer.

To gauge the sincerity behind a lot of elite leftist ideology, it's worth taking a look at people's "revealed preferences." Ideologies like antiracism and critical race theory hold that meritocracy, color blindness, equal opportunity, and the other values of Dr. Martin Luther King Jr. and the Civil Rights Movement all just act as a disguise for the true aim of white people, which is to continue subjugating Black people and other racial minorities. There is no doubt that the United States, like many countries, continues to suffer from open racial wounds, and that the African-American story has a unique place in American racial, social, economic, and political history. But if antiracism and CRT are correct about contemporary America—the United States in 2023—how do we explain the fact that the supporters and propagators of these ideologies have chosen to stay here? That there isn't a mass exodus of Americans with "oppressed blood" to foreign countries? And that the champions of these ideologies tend to be disproportionately represented in media, universities, NGOs, and other elite, high-paying institutions?

Further, how do we explain the fact that one of the fastest-growing immigrant groups in the United States is Black immigrants from Africa and the Caribbean? Estimated to be about 4.6 million in 2019, the surge in Black African and Caribbean immigration to America has resulted in the astonishing fact that one in ten Black Americans are now immigrants. These more recent Black Americans are not just here, they are quickly scaling the peaks of educational attainment and professional success. In fact, the most successful overall ethnic group in the United States today—by metrics ranging from educational attainment and lifetime earnings to divorce and birth rates—is none other than Nigerian Americans.

That's "voting with your feet," and leftist ideology has nothing to say on the subject.

THERE IS a silver lining in all this.

Leftist ideology in America (as distinguished from liberalism or liberal causes) has become so self-contradictory and patently absurd that ordinary citizens—especially parents—have shown signs of exiting from it completely. In January of 2022, the increasingly blue Virginia elected a Republican governor on the back of a controversy about whether or not parents should have the right to object to the teaching of leftist racial ideologies in public schools. Terry McAuliffe, the former governor of the state, had vetoed legislation that would have required schools to inform parents about new and controversial curricula. During the campaign, McAuliffe said: "I'm not going to let parents come into schools and actually take books out and make their own decision . . . I don't think parents should be telling schools what they should teach." Glenn Youngkin, the Republican candidate, ran on the idea that of course parents should be involved in their children's education. After Youngkin won the election, along with his Black Jamaican female lieutenant governor, Winsome Sears, and his Cuban attorney general, Jason Miyares, they were all referred to as "white supremacists" by MSNBC for advocating for the democratic concept of making schools accountable to their communities. But the common sense and ordinary decency of Virginia voters saw through the racialist, North Korean-esque attempt to paint any opposition to critical race theory as "oppressive."

Similarly, in February of 2022, voters of deep-blue San Francisco voted to recall all three members of the city's school board in a landslide. Supporters of the recall made up over 70 percent of the total vote, an astonishing majority. During the entirety of the pandemic, the school board had kept public schools closed to in-person learning, leading to dramatic learning losses for the city's poorest and most vulnerable students, while endlessly debating whether schools named after famous white supremacists like Abraham Lincoln should be renamed. The school board also ended test score criteria for the city's most prestigious and high-achieving public high school, Lowell, where Asian American students have been disproportionately represented— and were thus disproportionately penalized. San Francisco voters were willing to humor leftist ideology so long as it only impacted other people—but when it came for their children, they'd had enough.

I do worry for my son as he enters the New York school system, which is not distinguished for either its sanity or its ability to stay above the political fray. But I'm heartened by the example set by Virginia and San Francisco parents, who not only saw past the fraudulence of the American version of leftism, but demonstrated their continued faith in democracy itself, by showing up at the ballot box and taking personal responsibility for the direction of their communities. They were not satisfied with convenient explanations that some forces beyond their control were oppressing or victimizing them. They realized their own mistakes, took responsibility for them, and decided to make improvements.

So I hold out some measure of hope for my son and his generation as they enter their school-age years. One way or another, I'll ensure that he gets the education he needs and deserves.

What I feel I have less control over, however, is his safety—and mine.

7

Systemic Violence in the Windy City

I n the thirteen years I lived in North Korea, I never saw a map of the world. Nor did I ever learn about the different peoples of the world, other than the Japanese imperialists and American Bastards. So naturally, I had no idea how many countries, let alone ethnicities, actually existed on Earth. As far as I knew, North Korea was like the sun, the center of the solar system, and all other peoples revolved around it, unless like American Bastards, they'd been extinguished by God, Kim Il Sung.

Many moons later, when I learned about the countries of the world, the Earth, the solar system, the Milky Way galaxy, and the ever-expanding universe, I thought my brain was going to explode like a supernova. Imagine explaining to an alien from Mars what a fidget spinner is. That's what it's like trying to explain planetary systems to a North Korean.

There's a good reason for that, of course, beyond the shortcomings of North Korean education. What do the origins of matter and energy and theories of space and time matter to a human being whose stomach makes growling noises at night to warn her against falling asleep instead of finding a way to alleviate her impending starvation? When my body communicated to me this way, as it frequently did for the first half of my life, I often looked up to the sky and begged for mercy, hoping something, anything, up there could hear me. I would pray for a miracle, that somehow a door would open up in the firmament and someone would drop food, and it would land in my lap. This was my only relationship with the stars.

Nature itself, Earth's nature, was different. I didn't pray to it so much as I *envied* it. I envied the birds and mice, who with a flap of their wings or a scuttle of their feet could escape to China and easily find food. I was jealous of birds in particular. All children at some stage in their growing up wish they can fly, but it's the wish to transcend earthly life, to be more than human, like a comic book hero, or a Disney character. I wanted to fly so that I could be less than human, or what it means to be human in North Korea—more discreet, with greater freedom of maneuver, for no other reason than that it would allow me to find food, fly freely and look for something to eat.

When I came to America, there were many freedoms I grew to appreciate, but one of the first was my newfound freedom of *movement*. When I was hungry, I could just walk to the store; when I wanted to see friends or a new sight, I could take a train; when I wanted to explore other parts of the country, and meet other Americans, and see new vistas and landscapes, I could just hop in a car or board a plane. If you have never envied a bird, even a pigeon—which I suspect most people haven't—it's difficult to convey how special this freedom really is.

In the beginning of 2019, while still enrolled at Columbia as a senior, I exercised this freedom and moved with my husband to Chicago, Illinois. I had visited the Windy City many times prior to the move because my husband's job was based there. I'd also given birth to my son there.

After I moved to Chicago, some of my friends there and back in New York told me that I had to be careful in certain areas of the city. The "South Side" in particular was mentioned a lot, apparently because of a high crime rate. Even though I'd already spent three years in New York City, I still wasn't used to the idea that in the United States of America in the twenty-first century, there were certain places so dangerous that Americans themselves didn't feel safe going there. Others told me that while it wasn't exactly advisable to walk around on the South Side, it probably wouldn't be dangerous for me in particular, as the crime rate there consisted mostly of what local police and residents called, in an oddly callous formulation, "Black on Black" crime. For a city with a Black mayor, a 30 percent Black population (twice the national average), and a proud civil rights history, I thought it strange that people seemed to consider Chicago so dangerous *for Black people*. I also thought it strange that people spoke this way of one of the most progressive cities in one of the bluest states.

For the second semester of my final year in college, I commuted between Chicago, where my then-husband was running a company, and New York every week to finish my courses at Columbia. I still wasn't finding my education at Columbia very fruitful, but I remained determined to complete my degree, for the sole reason that one of my father's wishes was for me to get a higher education. For that, I was willing to continue putting up with all the ever-worsening woke propaganda nonsense for one more year. I was also told that a completed bachelor's degree would help me land a career in human rights activism.

I had originally considered such careers in international organizations like the United Nations, but I'd become increasingly disillusioned with their effectiveness—indeed, I could no longer understand the UN's purpose, or even its existence. To this day, the North Korean government retains full UN membership, meaning its vote in the General Assembly is worth the same as America's. It has been allowed to vote on human rights resolutions and chair committees on nuclear disarmament! Since 2005, the General Assembly has adopted a resolution every year to condemn the human rights situation in North Korea, but of course this has meant exactly nothing. Not a single victim of the Kim dictatorship has ever been helped by one of these meaningless resolutions, whose only purpose is apparently to allow self-admiring diplomats and bureaucrats to congratulate each other for being so virtuous.

Needless to say, I'd ruled out a career at the UN by the time I got my bachelor's degree in Human Rights with a concentration in Political Science from Columbia University. I wasn't able to attend the graduation ceremony, because there wasn't one. It was May of 2020.

The first wave of the pandemic was in full swing, and in America, New York City was ground zero.

BY FEBRUARY of 2020, like everyone else, I'd started to follow the bleak news. There was a novel coronavirus spreading around the world that originated in Wuhan, China. Even though it had appeared in Europe, too, and was starting to decimate parts of Italy, Americans were still being assured that it wouldn't come for us, that we wouldn't need to do things like wear masks or participate in lockdowns, which was what only poor or backward or overpopulated societies had to do. For me at the time, news of a viral pandemic did not even register as a potential hardship on the scale of many of the things I'd already been through.

Then in March, Chicago went into lockdown. On March 20, the mayor issued a shelter-in-place order. Schools and businesses were shuttered. Masks were still considered unnecessary at this point, and then it was considered selfish to purchase them if you weren't a health care worker, and then it was illegal to leave your house without one. Indoor spaces like grocery stores were kept open; outdoor spaces like playgrounds for children were closed. The government talked about the importance of "contact tracing," then never seemed to implement it. It also spoke of the need for widespread testing, but continued to make fast, easy, affordable, at-home testing virtually illegal for the first year by burying the companies that made them in regulatory hurdles. Americans accused each other of being traitors for either complying or refusing to comply with government orders, which themselves were changing from day to day. It was chaos.

As someone from East Asia, this was quite a spectacle to behold. Effective public health measures that proved quick, cheap, and relatively uncontroversial in South Korea seemed to tear America apart at the seams. In my building in Chicago, there were parents who would not let their newborn baby go outdoors, and kept her inside their apartment for more than a year.

The most notable aspect of the American response was how little sense it seemed to make, even as very little about the virus was known, including how it originated, how it made people sick, how it could be treated, and what its long-term consequences might be. China decided on a policy of "zero COVID"; countries like Sweden decided on a policy of herd immunity, or "let it rip." Whatever the advisability of these different strategies, they were at least consistent and comprehensible to the people who had to live under them. In America, by contrast, as the pandemic wore on, things only seemed to make less and less sense. As bars were reopened, public schools remained closed. As adults were permitted to un-mask, schoolchildren were forced to upgrade from cloth to medical-grade masks.

First businesses were shut, although they were apparently allowed to operate if they served dinner to California governor Gavin Newsom or styled House speaker Nancy Pelosi's hair or served cocktails to San Francisco mayor London Breed. Then the ones that hadn't gone bankrupt were allowed to reopen, but only at 25-percent capacity. Diners could remove their masks while eating and talking, but not while walking into or out of the restaurant. People were asked to stand six feet apart, then ten, and then nightclubs were reopened, and then closed back down, and then reopened again.

The only appropriate way to regard all this, I thought, was to just throw up your arms and laugh. It seemed to me that the American preference for dividing all cultural, social, and political issues into Left versus Right, Liberal versus Conservative, or Blue versus Red clearly didn't apply here. No one had any idea what they were doing, and very few of the people advocating in public for maximalist positions on one side didn't seem to live according to those positions in their own private lives.

And yet, the pandemic very quickly became a cultural and political dividing line for many Americans. It didn't help that it was also an election year, and Donald Trump was a highly polarizing president, inspiring either fierce loyalty or extreme hatred among voters eager to credit him with everything that went right or tar him with anything that went badly. America was like one giant, open, raw nerve.

And then, on May 25, 2020, less than a week after I graduated, a police officer in Minneapolis killed an innocent Black man named George Floyd.

THE PROTESTS that followed Floyd's murder resulted in consecutive nights of rioting and looting in Chicago between May 29 and June 1. Several small businesses and stores in downtown Chicago—including some on the Gold Coast and the "Magnificent Mile" on Michigan Avenue—were completely destroyed. Pharmacies, children's hospitals, and charities were among the buildings and storefronts burned and smashed. There were fatal shootings every night, and the sirens of police cars, fire trucks, and ambulances responding to emergencies never seemed to abate. Because of several threats that were made to the city's infrastructure, all the bridges over the Chicago River were lifted. Only one heavily guarded bridge connected my neighborhood in downtown to other parts of Chicago. During the day, we had to go through several checkpoints to make our way across the city; at night, there were curfews.

One day during the rioting, my husband went out to see what was happening firsthand. All along Michigan Avenue, only a block from our home, nearly every store was being looted or suffered an attempted looting. (Notable exceptions included Banana Republic and the Orvis fly fishing store.) Several police officers were standing outside while rampant theft was unfolding. The police were apparently under orders by the mayor not to stop the looters unless violent crimes were committed.

Although the atmosphere was largely jubilant and people seemed to be having the time of their lives, it was not safe to be outside. After hearing shots fired in one of the many nearby drive-by shootings that evening, my husband realized that it was probably not smart to remain outside, and he returned home. We were grateful that night to live on a high floor of an apartment building, out of the way of any bullets flying around. But the supermarket on the bottom floor was looted that evening. A couple of weeks later, only fifty-five yards away from our building, a Ronald McDonald House had its windows smashed. The "mostly peaceful" rioters didn't mind attacking a home where sick children were staying.

Because it was the week of my (virtual) graduation, my mother was visiting us from South Korea at the time. The sounds of the riots—which included not only the sirens of first responders, but windows breaking at the building across the street from mine— kept her up at night. During that whole week, my mother and I spent long hours watching coverage of the Chicago and national riots on local and national TV news, which I would translate for her. Anyone wondering about the utter strangeness of mainstream media coverage during this period need only have looked at my mother's face. As she saw images of buildings burning, windows being smashed, and merchandise being looted, I would translate the broadcast for her: "The nationwide protests for racial justice have been mostly peaceful, with the exception of a few bad apples and isolated incidents."

When she told me it reminded her of Korean Central Television, the main channel in North Korea, what was I supposed to say? At least I knew I wasn't alone in thinking that certain developments in the United States reminded me of my birthplace.

AGAIN, I know how absurd that can sound to American ears—and of course I don't draw a one-to-one comparison. Talk about "revealed preference" and "voting with your feet"—clearly, out of all the people in the world, I do not think that there are any equivalencies between America and North Korea! But because I love America so much, and because I'm committed to resisting any encroachments on its freedoms, I do draw on my knowledge and experience of North Korea to illuminate—not exaggerate—threats to liberty in America. And during the summer of 2020, it was hard not to notice American phenomena that reminded me of North Korea.

Consider what might be called the politics of emergency. Ever since the days of Kim Il Sung, the regime in Pyongyang has used the threat of internal and external enemies to justify the suspension of rights and the criminalization of dissent. In North Korea's revolutionary war for survival, free inquiry (or "counterrevolutionary thought") is not just unhelpful and irritating; as far as the government is concerned, it is seditious. A perpetual state of existential danger has meant that certain pillars of civilization—a free press, for instance, or the equal application of laws—must be understood instead as weapons that could harm the regime in its fight against American and Japanese imperialists. The Kim family and the substrata that make up the Korean People's Army and the Workers' Party of Korea—the North Korean elite—believe they have been summoned to act as guardians of this revolution, righting the course of history.

How did American elites behave during the election of 2020, an emergency if there ever was one? It was the final opportunity, as I recall, to remove the fascists in the White House, the Russian puppets in the Oval Office, the white nationalists putting babies in cages. And under such circumstances, truth in reporting was no longer seen as a democratic norm. As the Hunter Biden laptop episode proved, it was regarded as an unaffordable luxury in the face of an existential threat. The ruling elite of nearly every national institution—the press and universities, major corporations and tech companies, the civil service and national security agencies, NGOs and philanthropic foundations—saw the abandonment of such norms not only as justifiable, but as a patriotic duty. Because of the danger posed by a second Trump term, the effort to defeat him demanded loyalty and unanimity. The American elite believed they were summoned to act as guardians of the Republic, righting the course of history.

As with North Korea's politics of national emergency, the anti-Trump movement in the United States offered no real alternative to the threat it claimed to fight, it merely created an echo chamber in which the ruling class confirmed its fears of internal and external subversion. Russiagate in particular served a medicinal purpose, allowing the governing elite to blame a foreign enemy for their own incompetence and callousness, which had left them vulnerable to electoral defeat by a political novice. The eternal threat of American subversion, Japanese colonization, and a treasonous fifth column serves a similar function for the North Korean regime, which of course assumes no responsibility for the many horrors it causes.

And if the "emergency" in North Korea can never be allowed to subside—lest the state lose its justifications for the permanent suspension of liberty—the American ruling class is also averse to letting good crises go to waste. Hence, when the Russiagate narrative collapsed, the anti-Trump coalition found a new way to maintain the state of emergency: racial wars, police brutality, and the various fronts of the woke war.

Here especially, parallels to North Korea are enlightening. Critical race theory and antiracism share with Marxism-Leninism (and *Juche*, its North Korean offshoot) an arcane vocabulary and impenetrable set of ideas that serve less as a tool of political change than as a social sorting mechanism that keeps the governing class as separate as possible from ordinary people. In America after the murder of George Floyd and the Black Lives Matter revolution that followed, the elite started to force ordinary people and employees to take part in "diversity training" in order to internalize the official ideology of wokeism as a condition of education and employment. (In Mao's China, these spectacles, in which ideological enemies were publicly humiliated and accused of crimes they didn't commit, were called "struggle sessions" or "denunciation rallies.") They also used it to cancel and de-platform political and ideological dissidents on social media and elsewhere. In order to survive, American students and employees were told they needed to master this increasingly complicated set of rules, exceptions, and quirks of ideology and language.

The official American progressive ideology that went into overdrive in the summer of 2020 also shared with its North Korean counterpart a certain wild disingenuousness. In North Korea, it is not uncommon to see the well-fed son of a Party official lambast a farmer on the brink of starvation for insufficient loyalty to the Dear Leader. In America's "racial reckoning" of 2020, it suddenly became possible, for example, for a white magazine editor to lecture a Black construction worker who planned to vote for the wrong presidential candidate for his "internalized racism."

Along these lines, "wokeness" now appears to be just an obnoxious rhetorical style that helps cover for something else: a coercive system administered by governing elites that demands adherence to an ever-expanding corpus of basically random sets of laws and regulations designed to keep the lower classes in check.

If that doesn't remind you of the communist dictatorship in North Korea, I don't know what would.

I HAVE one more story to tell from that summer in 2020. It was the seminal event in my life in America, and in many ways forms the basis of my motivation for writing this book.

On August 14, it was a beautiful day in Chicago, and I decided to take a walk down Michigan Avenue with my two-year-old son and our nanny, a young Muslim woman who wears a hijab. We'd spent a lot of time indoors by that point, and I wanted my son to go back out in the world and get some fresh air.

At a little after 4 p.m., just a block away from Jane Byrne Park on the Magnificent Mile, I noticed that people were following me closely behind. When I turned around to look, I saw two women. They immediately cornered me, and one of the women shoved me into a marble pillar on the outside of a building. As she held me against the pillar the other woman fished through the purse I was holding for my wallet, and then punched me hard in the chest. When I tried to call the police, one of the women knocked my phone out of my hand and threw it into the street. I reached out to hold the arm of one of the women and started to yell for help, screaming to my nanny to take my son inside the nearby Macy's. He'd seen the woman punch me and looked really scared.

When they got off of me and started to make off with my wallet, I went into the street to retrieve my phone and started recording them as they walked away, shouting that I'd just been robbed. One of them turned around as I was recording her and screamed that by trying to call the police and recording her, I was being racist. "A person's skin color doesn't make them a thief!" she shouted at me. A woman on the sidewalk, who appeared to be nothing but an ordinary bystander, apparently heard her and started screaming "Racist!" at me, repeatedly. The two women who robbed me were both Black.

Michigan Avenue is an extremely busy and crowded street, and the altercation caused quite a scene, but by this point it took on a very specific and shockingly absurd valence. Several bystanders, seemingly of all races, started shouting at me. I remember in particular a white woman standing at a bus station with teenage children (presumably they were hers), saying loudly to them while looking at me that they were witnessing racism in action.

After I'd called the police, they arrived within thirty minutes and generously offered me medical attention, which I politely declined. They told me I was lucky not to have been stabbed or shot, and that I should never, ever fight back in situations like this, because life itself is more important. They took my statement, and later had me pick one of the assailants—the one who'd punched me—out of a lineup after having tracked her down. (After the altercation she proceeded to use my credit card in taxis and retail stores, leaving an obvious trail for the police to follow.) I decided to press charges against her. It turned out that she'd had several prior convictions, including aggravated battery, and pleaded guilty to a charge of unlawful restraint. As part of the plea agreement, prosecutors dropped the robbery count, and in exchange she was given a two-year prison sentence. The tabloid the *Daily Mail* eventually ran a story on the incident, including the name and photos of the assailant. I was told this was not ideal, as "revenge crime" and "revenge murders" are not uncommon in Chicago.

To this day, I don't know why, of all the many people on Michigan Avenue that day, they targeted me. Given all the other physical attacks on Asian Americans that surged that summer—again, according to the most recent crime data, about a quarter of the violent attackers were Black, about a quarter were white, a quarter Latino and "other" combined, and a quarter Asian—I suppose it's no great mystery. What I still can't understand is the behavior of the bystanders, none of whom thought to even vocally defend a young mother being assaulted in the street in front of her son, choosing instead to yell nonsense at her and egg on the attackers. For me, it was a sign of how far advanced the woke disease really was in America by that point, and how inhumane it was making otherwise normal people. This is the only contribution of the woke movement to American life: to reduce human beings to the color of their skin and determine whether or not they're deserving of help, dignity, or physical safety on that basis. It would make the American heroes of the Civil Rights Movement turn in their graves. It's why I wrote this book.

8

What's Yours Is Mine

When I first visited America back in 2013, one of the most striking things to me was the country's astonishing degree of *abundance*. Even in the relatively small city of Tyler, Texas—population 106,000, making it just the thirty-third biggest city in Texas and the 299th in the United States—there were stores and businesses everywhere hawking all kinds of goods and services. Everywhere I looked there were new and neat-looking products, perfectly packaged and labeled, ready for purchasing, ready for consumption. If toward the end of a business day a store was running low on some product, by early the next morning it was fully stocked again, as if by magic.

In North Korea, we had *jangmadang* (black markets), where we were lucky to find a few bare necessities like dried food, or luxury goods like Chinese knockoff sneakers and handbags. Even after my escape and eventual move to South Korea, in a typical store in Seoul I might have found one or two different options for a particular type of product. In

America, however, for each specific product there seemed to be virtually *unlimited* options. In a typical big-box grocery story—not a fancy, niche organic food store, just your typical HEB supermarket—there were over a dozen *different* types of apples, all with sweet-sounding names: Honeycrisp, Gala, Pink Lady, Fuji, Granny Smith. For packaged products, like toothpaste, it seemed as though every company sold different types for different people with different tastes at different stages of their lives. In America, I learned, there's no such thing as just a "toothbrush." There is soft, medium, and hard bristle; electric and manual; kids and adults; boy and girl; Star Wars and Toy Story. At times, the sheer number of choices overwhelmed me. What if I made the wrong decision? Or just a suboptimal decision? I wasn't used to having to make so many different decisions so often throughout a typical day.

I also didn't understand the reason for the existence of many of the products I saw for sale. It had never occurred to me that fruit needed to be peeled, and that this could be done with a *fruit peeler*, or that food shouldn't be cooked in a bowl or on a plate but in a *cast-iron Crock Pot*. I have since reversed my position on these products, by the way, and now enjoy them both! And that's the genius of capitalism. The secret behind all these seemingly silly products is that they wouldn't exist in the first place unless they were meeting a need that ordinary people actually have. A demand exists in the market, producers meet that demand, and consumers benefit. A supply chain is set up, each node along it is compensated for its role, and businesses profit from the margin between the retail price and the cost of goods sold. An entire economic value chain, millions of little microeconomies, beautifully on display in every aisle and on every shelf of an American storefront.

The existence of multiple products in each category also meant that there was plenty of *competition* to fulfill the needs of American consumers. Most brands clearly competed with each other based not only on price but also on perceptions of quality, or additional features, or tactics, like savings through bulk purchasing. I later learned by reading books by the eighteenth-century Scottish economist Adam Smith, the "Father of Capitalism," that all this was made possible by the division of labor and workforce specialization. One person makes the aluminum blade, another makes the plastic handle, another makes the rubber grip around the handle—and voilà, you have a fruit peeler, which is picked up from the manufacturer by yet another person and delivered to the store, where it's sold to a consumer. No one person is responsible for everything, but everyone's responsible for something. This process is the exact opposite of *Juche*, the official North Korean ideology of "self-reliance," in which everyone is supposedly responsible for doing everything themselves. In reality, of course, *Juche* means that nothing works, and everyone's hungry.

Trade is another obvious element of any American store. There are not only innumerable American goods, but goods from all over the world. If price is your biggest constraint, you can buy a product from Vietnam; if quality is your biggest concern, you can buy from Germany; if local sustainability is an important value to you, you can buy from North America. Whatever your priorities and needs, there are products available to you.

As I spent more time in America, and especially in New York—a melting pot of immigrant communities from all over the world—I learned that capitalism doesn't just fuel the United States, it powers the entire world. Capitalism doesn't just make products available to consumers, it has lifted billions of human beings out of poverty and starvation. It is also the most democratic and just system that human beings have so far invented. In a capitalist society, every consumer "votes" by spending their hard-earned money on the things they prefer—often far more indicative of their actual, deeply held preferences than the way they vote at a ballot box. If you don't support child labor, for instance, you can refuse to purchase products that were made by children; if you want to support certain types of farming or manufacturing, you can buy products from companies that practice them; if you want to support an embattled foreign country, you can buy their imports.

In a socialist system, no one has any of these powers. In a socialist system, even if you don't support slave labor, or inhumane working conditions, or unfair pay for working people—well, tough luck, because under socialism, you don't have a choice in anything. There's no way to change any of it, because the only items available for purchase are the ones the regime has chosen for you. In fact, the absence of capitalism and free markets makes it virtually impossible for societies to change at all, except through brute violence.

I've come to believe that only through capitalism can we establish a more just and humane society. If more people choose to buy meat from animals that were treated humanely, for example, or products free from the use of modern-day slaves in the supply chain, we can actually make the world a better place through small, individual decisions that amount to massive reform. This is the beauty of capitalism, and no other social or economic system can claim it—including (and often especially) socialism.

In North Korea, very few capitalist concepts even exist (the Kim regime bans the word *profit*, for example). But the ones that do exist demonstrate how much more natural they are to human nature than any of the other ideological alternatives. This is best understood in the existence in North Korea (like in every other society that has ever existed) of an underground economy, where human beings intuitively understand how to trade and barter like perfect capitalist merchants and captains of industry. My father was assigned a factory job in Hyesan that was a complete dead end, as the factory was defunct and didn't actually produce anything beyond carbon emissions. My father, always thinking first about putting food on the table for his wife and daughters, made the incredibly risky decision to start trading for himself. First he bought and sold dried fish and cigarettes. When the margins weren't profitable enough, he started moving metals and smuggling them into China instead. This turned out to be a lucrative but highly dangerous business, and for a period of time, our family did well by North Korean standards.

After my father's arrest, our fortunes of course took a dramatic turn for the worse. I was about eleven years old when I decided to follow in my father's footsteps and trade.

As I recounted in *In Order to Live*, my mother loaned me some seed money to start my own business. I used it to buy some rice vodka to bribe the guard at a state-owned orchard that grew persimmons. After accepting the vodka, he let me and my sister sneak into the orchard to pick some fruit. We filled a big metal bucket with persimmons and carried them for miles back to Kowon, where I sold them in the *jangmadang*, the markets that popped up all over North Korea during the devastating famine in the 1990s.

"These are the most delicious persimmons!" I cried out to the customers as they walked by. "Buy them here!" After a few weeks, I had enough money to pay back my mother, buy some candy, and buy another bottle of rice vodka to bribe the guard again. It was genius!

I was eleven and had no education, and yet being an entrepreneur came naturally, as it does to many people, if given the freedom to do it. During those days, I would spend hours thinking of schemes to bribe other guards at other farms so that I could diversify my inventory, and sell more goods to more people and make more money.

My career as a persimmon saleswoman and vodka procurer was ultimately short-lived, since our shoes eventually wore down from all the walking in the orchard and my mother could not afford to buy us new pairs as frequently as we would need them. Still, I learned something important from my short time as a market vendor: *Once you start trading for yourself, you start thinking for yourself.*

And that is why capitalism is so inimical to authoritarianism. Self-professed enemies of capitalism claim that their opposition is to inequality, or to injustice, or to exploitation—all of which of course are worse in socialist systems than in capitalist ones. But the true aim of anticapitalism is not justice or social betterment—it is to narrow the boundaries within which people are capable of thinking for themselves. The freedom that capitalism grants to individual human beings to think and act for themselves, thereby accumulating wealth, is the reason it is under increasing suspicion in America today.

ONE OF the most influential economists of the twentieth century was the University of Chicago scholar Milton Friedman, winner of the Nobel Prize in Economic Sciences in 1976. Friedman once wrote that "the only cases in which the masses have escaped grinding poverty, are where they have had capitalism and largely free trade." This is true even of countries like communist China, where the narrow, limited introduction of capitalism and free markets after the Cultural Revolution was able to lift hundreds of millions of people out of poverty and illiteracy. It was true of the Central and Eastern European states that at last were free to throw off the yoke of the Soviet Union after 1990, becoming rich and prosperous nations. And it is true of the United States, the wealthiest country in human history.

It may not be immediately obvious to anyone who's had to file business taxes with the IRS or obtain various business licenses from America's innumerable regulatory agencies, but the United States is exceptionally pro-business, especially when compared with the rest of the world. Regulations are cumbersome and not all the incentives are perfectly aligned, but no economic system in the world is more favorable to entrepreneurs—that's why more innovators, creators, and dreamers immigrate to America than to any other country. (If you know anyone who thinks that America is uniquely bigoted and xenophobic, just ask them to explain why the United States gets more visa, green card, and citizenship applications than any other country in the world.)

There are people in America today who think that "business" and "investing" are somehow synonymous with "fraud." These people don't understand that to be an entrepreneur is not to simply think of a novel way to profit, like bribing your way into an orchard and selling the fruit back to shoppers. It is a way of identifying a deep human need and figuring out how to meet it, thereby creating products and services and jobs for other people—people who may one day have an idea of their own, and who in almost all circumstances have their own families to feed, houses to build and buy, and taxes to pay. *Of course* successful entrepreneurs should be rewarded with the monetary profits of the social goods and services they create, whether those rewards are in the millions or billions.

To someone like me who was born in North Korea, but also to

billions of other people around the world, the values of entrepreneurship, free enterprise, starting a business, and doing well are sacred—and there is no limit to how much good they can do. They are also *incredibly* complicated and sophisticated! For a North Korean immigrant, learning how the New York Stock Exchange works is like learning fifth-dimensional string theory. One of the main reasons why I studied economics at Columbia was to learn as much about modern economics, business, and finance as I could in the shortest amount of time.

That's why it's been so troubling to see these basic values come under attack in America. (Though I've noticed that the attacks come predominantly from very comfortable and well-fed professionals with advanced degrees, seldom from lower- or working-class people.) Self-identified socialists in state and federal government and elsewhere criticize the American system for being too favorable to what they called the "millionaire class" when I first came to America, and which they now call the "billionaire class." (Perhaps too many of them are millionaires themselves, now?) They apparently don't see the United States as the predominately middle-class country it is (it is estimated that somewhere between 50 and 65 percent of Americans live in middle-class households), but as a caste system in which it's possible to accumulate wealth only through privilege and systemic abuse of the lower classes, never through hard work or innovation. New York congresswoman Alexandria Ocasio-Cortez said it best when she claimed in 2020 that "no one ever makes a billion dollars; you *take* a billion dollars." I suppose when Ms. Ocasio-Cortez buys an iPhone, rents a Toyota, searches on Google, and posts on Instagram, all those companies are simply *taking* her (taxpayer-funded) salary away? I don't suppose she's happily *paying* them for the goods and services she enjoys?

People ideologically aligned with Ocasio-Cortez and others like her often cite the vulnerability of capitalist economic systems to political lobbying, and thus corruption. This is, at best, 99 percent wrong. *All* economic and political systems are susceptible to corruption—but only capitalist systems are capable of self-correction. The railroad lobby was influential until the invention of the car. The coal lobby was vastly more influential before the invention of hydraulic fracking. The oil and gas lobby will become less effective once we innovate our way to cheap, high-quality green technologies. If you attempt to tamp down innovation and markets, you don't get *less* lobbying—you only cement in the advantages of those who got there first, thereby worsening corruption.

Capitalism has many flaws, but in three hundred years no society has come up with a better alternative, and no one who isn't a college student, a university professor, or a politician—as far as I can tell—is actually clamoring for anything else. The fact is, no ethical, law-abiding American should ever have to be apologetic about their success—and the vast, vast majority of American success stories are indeed built on the ethical treatment of workers and compliance within the boundaries of the law. Nor is anyone in America forced to work a job they don't want, or keep a job they don't like. The government cannot compel you to start a business—though unfortunately, as we discovered during the pandemic, politicians hostile to business and enterprise can try to force you to close them.

HERE'S ANOTHER Milton Friedman quote I love: "A society that puts equality before freedom will get neither. A society that puts freedom before equality will get a high degree of both." What Friedman meant was that societies that prioritize equality never bring the people on the bottom to the top, but force everyone down as low as possible, where they can all be equal—this is the essence of socialism. Societies that prioritize freedom, on the other hand, naturally result in a much higher degree of actual equality than the socialist system. What is preferable: a society in which there is great inequality between the average person, who makes $65,000 per year, and the top 1 percent, who make $500,000 per year—or a society in which everyone is equal . . . at an annual income of $4,000?

The answer is obvious, but the "wealth gap" is still demonized in America, as if the space that allows for upward mobility should itself be shrunk, leaving no room whatsoever for each generation to do better than the last. Coercive efforts to narrow the wealth gap—which amount to using the tax code to disincentivize business creation and hiring—are advocated for in the name of "equality" or "equity," but produce neither. This is of course because punitive taxation does not in any way power greater economic growth—it merely shifts economic gains from private citizens to the government. It would be one thing if the U.S. federal government were a responsible steward of our tax dollars and used them to build world-class transportation, public safety, education, and health care systems. But the U.S. government certainly does not.

It would also be one thing if this anticapitalist sentiment were new and untried, and we had no examples to point to in order to understand how it has worked in the past. But these ideas are decades and centuries old, and have failed everywhere they've been tried. It's not just the current and former communist countries—after World War II, Israel, India, and even the United Kingdom all tried socialist economic models with disastrous results. The fact that all three are now engines of economic growth and wealth creation is only due to their introduction (and in some cases reintroduction) of free markets.

Anticapitalists and socialists everywhere know this history as well as anyone, so what do those in America actually want to do with the economic reforms they propose? In case it isn't obvious already, I believe strongly from my eight years in the United States that the elite of this country do not care much for the lower, working, or middle classes. The so-called economic reforms, business regulations, and tax increases that have been passed in the last several years have, from what I can tell, accrued no benefit whatsoever to people who actually depend on social services like public schools, universities, hospitals, parks, and transportation. With every new tax increase, with every new federal regulation, with every new piece of legislation, it seems that bad schools remain bad, unaffordable health care remains unaffordable, and dangerous neighborhoods remain dangerous. This suggests that the priority is never to actually *improve* the lives of individual people and families, but to simply increase the *number* of people who depend on new and existing government programs because they have nowhere else to turn. In other words, the solution to a bad hospital isn't a good hospital, it's two bad hospitals.

This problem is, unfortunately, most evident in the cities dominated by a Democratic political machine—cities with endemic corruption and that effectively have no political opposition. Less surprisingly, it is most evident in cities with public officials who profess to in some way be socialist or anticapitalist. New York, Chicago, Los Angeles, San Francisco, Detroit, Baltimore—it never quite works out that the bluer the city hall or the bluer the mayor's mansion, the better the schools or the lower the crime.

And the bluer the city government, the bleaker the prospects for hope. In a city like Chicago with a disastrous public school system, an innovative, entrepreneurial idea like charter schools faces immediate and crushing opposition from teacher's unions. In a state like California, creative medical innovations or solutions to the epidemic of homelessness are immediately crushed by public health and environmental bureaucracies. Keep them in the public schools, keep them in the public hospitals, keep them dependent on the government bureaucracies, and narrow all private options—that seems to be the program.

This need to keep and accumulate as many citizens as possible who are dependent on the state also helps explain the overlap between people who are hostile to capitalism and people who are hostile to family life. The family remains the foundation of American society, the single most important institution in the life of children, far more so than any government agency dedicated to child education or welfare. But for decades now, the American family has been suffering. Absent fathers, children born out of wedlock, and the destructive effects of drug and alcohol abuse have eroded the central role of the family in American life.

"We know that more than half of all black children live in single-parent households, a number that has doubled—doubled—since we were children. We know the statistics—that children who grow up without a father are five times more likely to live in poverty and commit crime, nine times more likely to drop out of schools and 20 times more likely to end up in prison. They are more likely to have behavioral problems, or run away from home or become teenage parents themselves. And the foundations of our community are weaker because of it."

That was not an arch-conservative or Republican. That was Barack Obama speaking on Father's Day in 2008. Then-senator Obama was describing an objective moral tragedy. But what he must have known from his time as a community organizer in Chicago was that this moral tragedy is not necessarily a problem for the state. In fact, it's an opportunity: The destruction of the family creates more government clients.

MY CONCERN with wealth is part of a larger question, the one that has preoccupied me since I left North Korea and finally found freedom. It is the question of national prosperity. How do nations achieve success—real economic, scientific, and cultural wealth? There's an example from history that I think points toward a possible answer.

History buffs know that one of the most impressive empires ever built was the Mongol Empire in the thirteenth century. The Mongols stretched from the Pacific Ocean in the East all the way to the Black Sea and Central Europe in the West. They conquered all of modern-day China and much of Russia in the north and moved south all the way to the Indian subcontinent—an estimated land grab of 24 million square kilometers at its fullest extension, equivalent to the size of the United States, Brazil, and Australia combined. This incredible feat of imperial expansion was achieved not by technological superiority, which fueled the European imperial project that began in the seventeenth century, but by uneducated tribesmen traveling on horseback and living in yurts.

How did such a primitive civilization manage to overwhelm and dominate sophisticated ones like Persia and Byzantium? In one word: meritocracy.

Genghis, the Great Khan of Mongolia, established a promotional system that was free from tribal association and the nepotism of the past. What Genghis valued above all was talent, work ethic, and dedication to the cause—not lineage, pedigree, or connections. To Genghis, there were far too many high-ranking officials who had made it to the top simply through their bloodline or corrupt practices like gifts, favors, and bribery, and ended up as incompetent, deadweight loss. He relentlessly cracked down on corruption and brutally executed officers he saw as insubordinates or weaklings.

I, of course, don't advocate for brutally executing anybody—nor for rape, pillaging, or imperial conquest. What I do think is important is that the idea of meritocracy being crucial to national survival and prosperity is an ancient one. While leftists in America routinely criticize merit itself as being somehow synonymous with racial privilege, even the Chinese Communist Party has embraced it with open arms, making entry into the civil service and appointments and promotions based on rigorous testing. From running health care in a village, to managing foreign investment in a city district, to supervising in a state-sponsored company, the provision of public goods is seen as requiring demonstrable talent, hard work, and dedication. Once a year in China, performance is reviewed through comprehensive interviews conducted by superiors, peers, and subordinates, who vet workers' personal conduct and conduct public opinion surveys to assess their competence.

These are for jobs in the Chinese bureaucracy—ordinary civil service positions, like those you'd find at the DMV. But to the Communist Party, competence in public administration is not merely a luxury anymore—it is the means to national prosperity, and thus a strategy for survival.

The dirty secret about left-wing attacks on capitalism, the family, and meritocracy in America is that they're regarded as quite the hilarious joke in China—which is happy to watch Americans devalue and degrade every source of strength they have.

PART III

THE FRAGILITY OF FREEDOM

9

The Terror of Cancel Culture

In August of 2020, I started a YouTube channel, *Voice of North Korea by Yeonmi Park*, to share my ideas about and research into the conditions of North Korea, and into China's role as the enabler and underwriter of the Kim regime. When I launched the channel the pandemic was in full swing, with millions of people still in some version of lockdown, and so online engagement was remarkably high. In less than two months, 100,000 users subscribed to the channel. This is what I had long wanted: not to fly to different conferences and private events at which I could grab only a moment of time from a small handful of powerful people, but a global platform that would connect me directly to a large audience of people all around the world. In my first half-decade in America, I'd discovered that trying to use my own personal story to influence the actions or behavior of decision-makers was a dead end. Real change has to happen through mutual education and engagement among lots of ordinary people. This was the original promise of the internet, and my idea was to use it to build an "army of kindred spirits" who would fight against the evil of these twin communist regimes.

I began with mostly descriptive and human-interest videos: ten-to-fifteen-minute segments on food in North Korea, the culture shock I'd experienced in America, introducing viewers to other North Korean defectors, and the like. Then I started to make videos introducing the audience to the North Korean regime itself: an explainer on the country's gulag system, a segment on Kim Jong Un's ruthless and mysterious sister, and a video on how the regime earns revenue. One video I made in September of 2020 on Ri Sol Ju, Kim's wife and North Korea's first lady, eventually earned three million views. Another I made in October, "Daily Life of a North Korean," received almost six million views. The channel really seemed to be taking off, and I saw in it a way to both broaden my activism and earn a modest living by monetizing the videos through advertisements.

But as fall turned to winter that troubled year, something shocking happened. I started to make videos not only about North Korea itself, but about Chinese complicity in the North Korean regime, and about the treatment of North Koreans—especially women—living in China. Each one of these videos was swiftly demonetized by YouTube. I made videos about the Chinese threat to global security, and about the questions surrounding the origins of COVID-19—YouTube demonetized these, too. Even a video I made about the Second Amendment—which had nothing to do with China at all—was demonetized. I also noticed an increasing number of friends and fans telling me that my Instagram account, which I used to keep people abreast of my activism, book tours, and collaborative efforts, was potentially being shadow-banned—meaning it was often difficult to find my account even if you searched for it by name.

At the same time, it was hard not to notice that several YouTube and Instagram accounts that, in one way or another, were obsessively dedicated to absolving the Chinese government of all wrongdoing during the pandemic, and that accused anyone who disagreed of being racist, were not only allowed to continue posting—their content was continually promoted on both platforms, and presumably received truckloads of ad revenue.

Until this point, the censorship I'd observed and in some cases experienced in America was what you might call "censorship lite." It mostly consisted of immature college professors and hysterical college students shouting other people down, but exercising no real power if you had the courage to stand up to them. "Hard censorship"—forcibly depriving someone of their living, or making their creative output disappear without any charge or trial or explanation—was a different matter entirely. It seemed so unthinkable to me that something like this could be possible and so routine in America that I figured I'd accidentally done something illegal, or broken a law without intending to.

But only a couple of months later, when the president of the United States was kicked off Twitter and virtually every other social-media platform—even if it was for challenging the results of the election or for appearing to put the peaceful transition of power into question—I knew it probably wasn't just me.

SPEAKING TRUTH to power is as old as America itself.

The United States might have been born as a reaction to monarchical tyranny in the late eighteenth century, but its deepest roots reach back a century and a half earlier. The English religious exiles who chose to make the difficult and dangerous journey across the Atlantic to the New World did so in search of greater individual and communal liberty—it was an exodus in search of truth and freedom. The sacrifices they made for the sake of that search were almost unfathomable. They left behind everything they ever knew and embarked on an entirely uncertain path. When they arrived in Massachusetts, the winter was unimaginably harsh, and the landscape of thick woods and forests was unforgiving. There was no obvious source of food or shelter; there were no authorities and there was no security. Everything had to be built from scratch.

Our forefathers in America were willing to undergo such extreme conditions and assume such dangers—all for the sake of freedom of religion. That's how precious they considered the basic freedoms of speech, expression, and conscience. They were willing to risk everything for it. This value was, of course, eventually enshrined into law in the form of the First Amendment to the Constitution in 1791. And for the vast majority of American history, it performed its function well.

I remember the shock of learning about the Skokie case of 1978, when the National Socialist Party of America—a neo-Nazi group—planned to march through the Chicago suburb, where many Holocaust survivors lived. Disgust at these latter-day Nazis and their horrible intention to insult Jewish survivors of the actual Nazi horror understandably led many Americans to believe that the planned march had to be stopped—that the police had to prevent them from organizing in the streets. But the American Civil Liberties Union (ACLU) understood that the First Amendment allowed the freedom of peaceful assembly, no matter the content. In fact, this was the same law that was used to defend the right of civil rights protestors to march through the South. The ACLU—a progressive legal organization, which in fact was led by several Jewish Americans—defended the First Amendment rights of the National Socialist Party of America, and won the case in the Supreme Court. The ACLU understood that no right is more sacred than the right to free speech, no matter the consequences.

Does anyone believe that the ACLU, or any other organization like it, would do the same today? Far from maintaining an absolutist commitment to the sanctity of freedom of expression, a large segment of American society now believes that free speech is a public and private threat. The right to not feel offended, the right to be protected from unpleasant realities and difficult ideas, the right to feel safe from people who disagree with you—these are of course not rights at all, but they have come to supplant the legal rights enshrined in the First Amendment.

And because no American is actually entitled to deny any other American their First Amendment rights under the law, many have come up with an extralegal strategy for suppressing speech they don't like: what is known as "cancel culture."

Most Americans understand cancel culture as the attempt to damage the reputations of famous people or destroy the careers of celebrities—J.K. Rowling for her views on gender, for example, or Dave Chappelle for his jokes about trans culture. But these are only the most high-profile cases that serve as examples to society at large. The real power of cancel culture is the *fear* that it instills in the minds of millions of ordinary people, convincing them to think twice about expressing themselves freely or else risk having their lives destroyed by real and/or online mobs.

There is a term for making people second-guess every word or gesture for fear of losing their livelihoods. It's called "dictatorship of the mind." From its earliest days, the Kim regime understood that ordinary Koreans wouldn't be able to contextualize or understand their bondage if they were deprived of the language required to describe it. Thus, in official North Korean, there is no word for *tyranny, trauma, depression,* or *love*—there are only synonyms for "socialist paradise." And so millions of North Koreans might be hungry and scared, but they don't have the vocabulary to articulate or imagine a different way of living.

At the end of the day, this is the object of cancel culture in America: to deprive people of the right or ability to express thoughts that run counter to official narratives, so that eventually, they won't even know how. Threaten enough people with the destruction of their reputations and livelihoods if they criticize the wrong thing, and eventually they won't even know how to criticize it.

It's not hard to see why this type of informal censorship would be favored by many political and business elites. Say you're an American company with factories in China that depend on slave labor, or you're an American politician who supported and encouraged the offshoring of American manufacturing to China. You can't *literally* throw Americans in jail for criticizing you. But you can try to destroy the careers and reputations of people who do, in order to dissuade them from attempting criticism in the first place. So if an online mob decides it's "racist" to criticize the Chinese government—for covering up the origins of COVID-19, say—that redounds to your benefit, because you *want* people to be afraid of losing their livelihoods if they criticize or oppose your own policies or business model.

This helps explain why so many media outlets, universities, foundations, NGOs, politicians, and corporations all seemed to spontaneously converge on the same narrative about COVID: "It came from a wet market, not a lab leak, and any speculation to the contrary is racist, and racist speech is the equivalent of physical violence, so it must be banned." This was obviously patently absurd on its face—but it was effective in making people second-guess their own common sense, which told them that the virus probably leaked from the nearby virus-research lab, and think better of voicing their well-founded opinions out loud. Citing China's supposedly low but clearly dishonest official case rates was also effective in convincing Americans that Chinese public health measures that the Left favored, such as mass lockdowns, actually worked.

I didn't think better of it, and it got me in trouble. Attempts to cancel me didn't end with YouTube demonetizing my videos, or Instagram and Twitter seemingly shadow-banning my accounts—whether these decisions were made by human beings or by algorithms. As I became more publicly critical of the Chinese government—mostly for its role in the sexual enslavement of North Korean women, hardly a "controversial" position—there was increasing pressure for previously friendly organizations to shut me out, on the basis that I was *too* controversial.

Toward the end of 2021, for example, I was invited to give a speech on my experience growing up in North Korea at Samsung Semiconductor, Inc., a U.S. subsidiary of Samsung Electronics in San Jose, California. I accepted the invitation and was scheduled to speak there on January 25, 2022. On the invitation, which went out to two hundred or so Samsung employees, the speech topic was officially labeled "Yeonmi's story of escaping North Korea," and it was part of a series called "Speaker series hosted by Women in Samsung Electronics." It was a pretty routine affair.

On January 13, however, I received an email that the speech had been canceled. According to the email, the event coordinator at Samsung "had approval to book Yeonmi, but as the contract was being processed, an executive objected saying she would be too 'political' and it went up the chain and they are insisting that they need to cancel."

Needless to say, I was quite shocked that speaking about my own life to a group of people in California would be considered "too political." So I decided to look up Samsung Semiconductor, Inc. online, and on their website I found this:

> Through the Samsung Corporate Social Responsibility (CSR) program, we strive to create positive change around the world, focusing on the regions where our employees are located and where we conduct business. In Suzhou, China, Samsung has invested $2.11 billion in facilities, production and research development, and employs 2,132 workers locally. With an emphasis on youth education, sustainable development and environmental protection, our corporate citizenship projects address global societal issues by leveraging Samsung's expertise in technology, culture and innovation.

Ah, I thought to myself. *That's why*. Samsung has a multibillion-dollar investment in China. It was hard for me to avoid the impression that if I were to say out loud in front of their executives that, for instance, my mother and I were enslaved and raped in China, and that the Chinese authorities knew about it—indeed, that they facilitated and condoned it, and that this is happening right now to thousands of other North Korean girls in China—it might reflect badly on Samsung Semiconductor, Inc. Calling me "too political" is like YouTube determining that I'm "racist"—a way to shut down all conversation and label the things I say as beyond the pale. Regardless of the truth.

Things like this have happened a number of times since. I was scheduled to give a similar talk at the FBI's field office in Dallas, for instance, until shortly before the event, when the head of the diversity department (yes, the FBI Dallas office apparently has one of those) called to say the event was canceled—with no explanation.

HAVING SURVIVED various attempts at cancellation myself, I can attest that it is not just a fad or a silly new front in a childish culture war. With the use of modern technologies, cancel culture in America has made a significant amount of progress toward accomplishing what no democratic regime is capable of doing on its own, and what every dictatorial regime in history has mastered: making human beings with unfavorable opinions disappear with the push of a button.

Think about what it requires for a traditional democratic government to make someone disappear. First, a judge must be convinced to issue a warrant. If the warrant is granted, a police officer must be identified to make an arrest. Then he must find the individual, physically detain him, and place him in custody. Throughout this process, the targeted individual is presumed innocent until proven guilty, and granted the rights of an innocent person. Then he must be taken into a court of law. There he must be tried and prosecuted, during which he is entitled to his own defense. If he loses, the judge or jury must render a sentence, and the individual must be taken to a prison. Only at the end of that long and complicated process can we say that the "regime" made someone "disappear."

Dictatorships are subject to no such processes. As soon as an individual is considered objectionable or undesirable, it is only a matter of kidnapping or killing him, or robbing him blind. No questions asked. There is no warrant or trial, no judge or jury.

Now, consider my single video on criticizing the Chinese government—nominally considered an enemy regime of the United States. With no trial, with no judge or jury, with no verdict, and with no sentence—in a word, with no due process—YouTube demonetized the video. Instagram has ostensibly shadow-banned my account at times. Organizations that had invited me to speak about my own life suddenly revoked the invitations, on account of my undesirable opinions. No charge, no conviction, but nevertheless stripped of my right to earn my honest living—with the push of a button.

I ask you, dear reader, which does this remind you of more—the democratic process or the dictatorial one?

Cancel culture is not just about trying to punish comedians for making occasionally tasteless jokes (which it is their right to do), it is about locking ordinary citizens out of social participation if their opinions are considered "undesirable" by the media, corporations, and government. It is as serious as serious gets.

It's hard to say what we can do about this new marriage of corporate, financial, technological, and political power that threatens to supersede our judicial system. One is to hope for the invention and widespread adoption of more decentralized technologies that will wean us off our dependence on Big Tech. Another is to opt out of the Big Tech space completely—to leave Twitter, Facebook, and all the other platforms that facilitate the rule of the mob.

A more modest proposal is to recommit ourselves to the founding principles of our Founding Fathers and their forebears: to freedom of speech, expression, and assembly. This means doing what the ACLU did in Skokie, Illinois: prioritizing the law over our own feelings. And it means defending the rights of individuals—even ones we disagree with—from the mob.

In other words, we must take the path of resistance. Like the pilgrims, we must take the road that makes us uncomfortable, that is uncertain and frightening, if that's what the truth demands. Because that is the only road to freedom.

10

The People's Republic of Chains

The Chinese economic growth miracle of the last two decades is, without a doubt, one of the most impressive and consequential developments in modern international history. Nicknamed "the red dragon," contemporary China has become either the biggest or second-biggest power in global trade and commerce. An enormous amount of credit for this astonishing feat goes to the industriousness of hundreds of millions of ordinary Chinese people. But a large part of the explanation also lies in the squalid tactics of the regime. The Chinese Communist Party has locked in the country's manufacturing dominance not simply through innovation but through low-cost production made possible by pitifully low wages and horrifying working conditions. It has mastered large-scale, low-cost shipping not only through efficient logistics but by manipulating global supply chains—often illegally—to give China an edge over the United States, Europe, and other major markets. This combination has created a lot of global instability, but enough internal legitimacy to keep the regime stable. Since the 1980s, China has lifted more people out of poverty than the rest of the world combined.

China's international prestige comes from other sources, too. It remains a permanent member of the United Nations Security Council, one of only five countries in the world that wields a veto power over joint resolutions, thanks to being on the winning side of World War II. China is also at the forefront of science and technology. It is the global leader in payments, online retail, and infrastructure like high-speed rail, and will likely soon dominate consumer electronics. It also has a plausible chance of winning the race for predominance in artificial intelligence and quantum computing, which would certainly help buttress its skyrocketing military power. Chinese defense spending in 2021 totaled about $240 billion, second only to the United States, and its active military force—over two million—is the largest in history.

These are remarkable achievements for a country that refers to itself as a "unitary, single-party, socialist state"—a political and economic model that, outside of China, has an unbroken historical track record of failure, collapse, and defeat. And it's not as if China doesn't share the same shortcomings as all the other communist regimes that have come and gone.

In 2020, of all countries in the world, China ranked 177th for "freedom of the press" by the nonprofit Reporters Without Borders, outranking only Turkmenistan, Eritrea, and—you guessed it—North Korea. China also came in at #129 in the CATO Institute's 2020 Human Freedom Index, which measures seventy-six distinct indicators of personal and economic freedom. Looking at qualitative indices of freedom, the only countries that cumulatively scored the same as or worse than China were Iran, Iraq, and North Korea (the "Axis of Evil") plus Cuba and Turkmenistan. Even when it came to business and financial freedom, China ranked 107th in an index put together by the Heritage Foundation.

So how has China, in a few short years, become the second most powerful country on earth—and one of the most powerful in history?

TO UNDERSTAND and appreciate how we got to the increasingly Chinese-dominated world we live in today—which we and our children will likely be grappling with for the rest of our lives—it's worth taking a very brief look through Chinese history, which I first started to understand and appreciate by taking a course on it through Prager University.

Ancient China was responsible for some of the greatest innovations in the history of mankind—paper, printing, gunpowder, alcohol, tea, umbrellas, rockets, and paper money all trace their existence to Ancient China. The Silk Road was one of the most sophisticated and intricate trade routes in history, connecting all of Eurasia together into one giant landmass of economic activity and cultural exchange. When Marco Polo put China on European maps, it was not a case of an "advanced" civilization "discovering" a "primitive" one—quite the contrary. Marco Polo was bringing knowledge of one of the most advanced civilizations on earth to a comparatively backward Europe.

The early modern period, however, was not good for China. By the nineteenth century, the European colonial empires had far outpaced it by nearly every metric of power—economic, military, technological— and China fell prey to Western imperial ambitions. In the early twentieth century, China was a country with no economic or independent political future—almost the entirety of its gigantic population lived in abject poverty, and many were deliberately made into opium addicts by Western powers, including the United States. China during this period was reduced to little else besides a Western sphere of influence, with the British, Americans, Germans, Russians, French, Japanese, and others all jockeying for influence and control.

Chinese resentment at having their great civilization converted into a Western imperial playground resulted in the Boxer Rebellion between 1899 and 1901. As the traditional Chinese government faltered—its failure to cast out the foreigners causing it to lose all legitimacy—a group of revolutionaries with widespread public support began the Chinese Revolution of 1911, which replaced China's 2,000-year-old imperial system with the Republic of China, headed by Sun Yat-sen. In March of 1912, Sun resigned and was succeeded by Yuan Shikai, who attempted to reinstate an imperial system with himself as emperor, leading Sun to start one of China's first modern political parties, the Kuomintang (or KMT). Sun fought hard to establish a representative democracy, but was largely unsuccessful.

In 1917, China entered World War I on the side of the Entente (France, Britain, and Russia). China contributed to the alliance mostly by providing resources in the form of laborers who worked in allied mines and factories. Nevertheless, after the war, the victors' peace— the Treaty of Versailles—ignored China's pleas to end its nightmare of foreign control. Instead of ceding Chinese territory previously held by the defeated German Empire back to the Chinese themselves, for example, the treaty simply handed it over to Japan.

On May 4, 1919, three thousand Chinese students demonstrated in Tiananmen Square to protest the Treaty of Versailles. The May Fourth Movement was part of a larger cultural mobilization aimed at replacing traditional Chinese society and values with more contemporary and future-oriented ones, which included promoting scientific endeavors, improving literacy, and making political participation more egalitarian, or populist. It was out of the May Fourth Movement that the Chinese Communist Party was soon born.

During the 1920s, China was divided by a power struggle between the KMT and CCP. The KMT was then still in control of the majority of China, with a strong base in urban areas, while the CCP boasted small holdings in rural communities. By 1928, the CCP was virtually suppressed in China, and the country was more or less united under the KMT. But the CCP reemerged on November 1, 1931, when it proclaimed the Jiangxi Province as the Chinese Soviet Republic. The army of the Republic of China, under the leadership of General Chiang Kai-shek, tried to destroy the communist army in 1934, and ultimately failed. But the fighting did lead the CCP to flee northward in the Long March, a six-thousand-mile trek in which the communists relocated from southeastern China to the country's northwest.

Meanwhile, in 1931, Imperial Japan had invaded and occupied Manchuria in northeastern China and established a puppet state, known as Manchukuo. The war that broke out on July 7, 1937, between the Republic of China and Imperial Japan is considered by most historians to mark the beginning of World War II—not Hitler's invasion of Poland, which came over two years later. By 1939, Japan controlled most of the east coast of China, while Chiang blockaded the communists in the northwest region. By 1944, the United States intervened on behalf of nationalist China, but the nationalists remained weak due to so many years of war, occupation, economic trouble, and rising inflation.

In the aftermath of World War II, there was chaos and tumult in China as the struggle between the nationalists (KMT) and communists (CCP) broke out into four years of civil war. By 1949, the CCP, led by Mao Zedong, finally defeated the KMT, and China was at last—from that moment through to the present day—a communist state.

From his earliest days as head of the CCP, Mao promised the Chinese people—in a term that should now be familiar to you—a "socialist paradise." There would be no private companies owned by capitalist fat cats, no blood-sucking landowners abusing their laborers, no unemployment in the cities, no more hunger, and no more bloodshed. And indeed, Mao and the CCP nationalized every resource, eliminated private property, and confiscated land from private owners.

The result was one of the greatest human catastrophes in world history.

Between 1958 and 1962, China suffered what is still, to this day, considered the worst famine in human history. As a direct result of Mao's land and property policies—which were part of the Great Leap Forward—between 15 and 55 million people starved to death. In 1966, Mao and the CCP began the decade known as the Cultural Revolution, in which up to 20 million Chinese were murdered in the ostensible attempt to purge China of ideological opposition to communism and to Mao's absolute rule. By the time Mao died in September 1976, 90 percent of the Chinese population lived in abject poverty, making less than $2 a day, and almost everyone had lost a parent, grandparent, child, or sibling to famine or massacre. Even in the annals of international communism and fascism, which has seen monsters and mass murderers as evil as Hitler, Stalin, Pol Pot, and the Kims, Mao stands alone. It is estimated that Mao—his rule, his policies, his government, his leadership—is personally responsible for up to 78 million human deaths. "Socialist paradise."

Then came the miracle. Deng Xiaoping took over China after Mao, and instituted several capitalist reforms. He introduced limited free markets, opened the country to foreign investment, and allowed many people to choose what jobs they wanted and which ones they didn't. Over the ensuing decades, the freer and more open the Chinese economy became, the more China prospered, and the CCP regained its lost legitimacy. Three decades after Deng's rule began, close to one billion people were lifted out of poverty. Chinese cities became world-class, Chinese technology became advanced, and in sheer numbers, the Chinese middle class became the largest in the world.

Much of this growth continued in the early years of Xi Jinping, who in 2013 became China's "paramount leader"—the only man since Mao to hold all three titles of head of state, general secretary of the Chinese Communist Party, and chairman of the Central Military Commission—but in the last few years, growth has started to slow, with many predicting a downturn. Xi has sought to preserve the economic benefits of Deng's market reforms while reimposing Mao's centralized power and restrictions on free enterprise and speech, and reconverting China into a quasi–police state. The difference now is that Xi has access to technology that Mao never even dreamed of: Facial recognition, AI surveillance networks, mobile and internet monitoring, and social credit systems are being deployed to turn China, once again—and like every socialist paradise—into a prison. If Chinese citizens before Xi had only some of the freedom and liberties Americans enjoy under the Bill of Rights, they now have none. Even their freedom of movement—their right to buy a bus ticket to visit a family member—depends on their support for the regime.

MY MOTHER and I had the misfortune of being inmates in this prison when we were trafficked there from North Korea. I went to China because I was determined to find my sister, but also because I wanted the one thing that by itself could grant me a better life: a bowl of rice. In exchange for that pitifully modest luxury, I became a man's house worker and sex slave at the age of thirteen, and had to watch my own mother repeatedly pillaged by other men.

To this day it makes me physically ill to think about it. But the older I get, the more the sickness I experience has to do with the knowledge that it's still happening—right now, at this very moment, as you read these words—to scores of other women and girls in China. What gives their captives the power and control they need to keep them enslaved is a single threat: "If you don't do what I tell you, I will report you to the police."

That threat is eminently credible. The Chinese authorities are notorious among North Korean defectors for their hair-trigger willingness to send North Koreans back "home," where everyone involved—the girls, their captors, the police—knows they will end up in hard labor camps until they die, or else be executed on the spot. This is a deliberate policy decision by the Chinese authorities. If they ended it, the human traffickers and their clients would immediately lose their ability to enslave North Korean women. But they won't: It is an important component of bilateral relations between Beijing and Pyongyang, and although the Kim regime can prove an irritant to the CCP now and again, China has shown no real signs of letting go of its client state.

The special relationship between the two communist regimes— the CCP and the Kim family—began during the Korean War, when

China and Russia actively aided Kim Il Sung in order to "unify Korea" under the communist banner. Mao Zedong's son, in fact, was killed in action in 1950 during an American bombing raid. (Legend has it that despite a prohibition on cooking at night in order to avoid detection from the air, Mao stole eggs to make himself egg fried rice on the night he died, alerting U.S. bombers to his unit's location and contributing to their deaths. Nowadays, every year on the anniversary of Mao's son's death, rebellious Chinese internet users post recipes for egg fried rice in order to mock the government, which the authorities promptly remove.)

Accurate figures for Chinese aid and exports into North Korea are hard to come by, as the scale of North Korean dependence on its humongous neighbor is humiliating to anyone who actually thinks that the Kim regime has preserved any semblance of "self-reliance," or that the *Juche* is anything at this point beyond a practical joke. But estimates from the last decade show North Korea to be little more than a Chinese colony. Chinese aid in 2014 was about $4 billion (North Korea's entire GDP was about $28 billion in 2016), China seems to account for approximately 95 percent of all North Korea's imports, and China receives about two-thirds of North Korea's exports. Without China, in other words, the North Korean regime literally would not exist.

In exchange for its support of the Kim family, China receives only small amounts of ores and mineral fuels. So what's in it for Beijing? The fact is, the existence of North Korea is good for China. It serves as a geographic buffer between China and the U.S. military forces stationed in South Korea, and North Korea's nuclear weapons function as a reliable military deterrent to greater U.S., Korean, Japanese, and Australian action in the region. North Korea is also, according to some

Chinese officials and academics—and this is not a joke—an example of why communism is *superior* to capitalism and democracy.

CHINESE INFLUENCE and control, of course, extends far beyond its own neighborhood. Taiwan, Hong Kong, and Tibet are only the crisis points within China's immediate sphere of influence, and countries like North Korea are little more than territorial extensions of the Chinese state. The majority of Chinese economic and political influence is being extended much farther afield, to the copper mines of Africa and Latin America, the land routes of Central Asia, and the energy fields of the Persian Gulf. Vladimir Putin's ruinous war in Ukraine, and the resulting sanctions on Russia's economic system, have virtually ensured that the entire Russian Federation—the largest sovereign landmass in the world—will become a Chinese economic dependency.

It is concerning enough that so much of the Earth's surface and its population will be under the influence of a state dedicated to the overthrow of American power—what's more concerning still is the shape that new power will take. China may be one of history's most intense drivers of economic development, but it comes at a higher cost than even economic growth can justify. As many countries in Africa, the Balkans, and Latin America have started to learn, the spread of Chinese power across the world means the spread of environmental damage and exploitation, abusive labor conditions, ruinous debt accumulation, poor infrastructure, and sex trafficking. There is no doubt that, on net, the rise of Chinese hegemony represents a negative and threatening prospect for nearly every country in the world.

It is therefore incumbent on the world's only rival superpower, the

United States of America, to stop it. Unfortunately, in recent years, America has become compromised.

In 2020 alone, a year in which much of global trade was disrupted and GDP fell precipitously, the United States still managed to be the largest importer of Chinese goods in the world, sending the CCP a whopping $452 billion. The Chinese, moreover, have infiltrated American business and finance at nearly all levels, acquiring American companies, becoming the largest shareholders in many American industries, buying up American real estate, forcing the transfer to China of American technology, and luring away the vast majority of American manufacturing. In Chicago, where I live, the epidemic of high-rise luxury real estate construction—contributing to a city-wide housing shortage, price hikes, and a housing affordability crisis—has been driven in large part by Chinese investment.

The fact is, a large segment of America's elite classes and most productive industries have been purchased by the Chinese. Big Tech, Wall Street, Hollywood, and the universities are all dependent on Chinese money and markets to keep their profits trending upward. Their behavior in the last two decades closely parallels Russia in the 1990s, when under Boris Yeltsin a handful of oligarchs looted and sold off the country's resources to enrich themselves while ordinary Russian people were plunged into chaos and poverty.

The consequences of this were most visible during COVID-19, when nearly all U.S. corporations, universities, and media rushed to defend the actions and decision-making of the Chinese government, helping the CCP cover up the origins of the virus by deeming anyone who disagreed with the official Beijing line as a "racist" or "crackpot" or "conspiracy theorist." It also became painfully clear that U.S. industry had outsourced the most basic capabilities to China: America, the most technologically advanced industrial country in history, could not even make its own masks or ventilators.

Across two presidential administrations now, the United States has vowed to do something about the Chinese threat: to bring more American manufacturing and business back home; to bolster U.S. defense capabilities; to counter Chinese influence in the Pacific, Europe, and the Middle East; and to stop the illegal Chinese practices of stealing trade secrets, forcing technology transfers, investing through shell companies, and integrating the use of slave labor into global supply chains. But both the Trump and Biden administrations have fallen far short. The fact is, America's China policy is not even really made by the American president anymore. It is made by the lobbying and interest groups and oligarchical classes that are dependent on the Chinese market, regardless of the effect on ordinary American workers and consumers.

The only hope for countering the spread of Chinese influence is the United States, but American elites are busy dismantling the sources of American economic and military power to the benefit of the Chinese in order to enrich themselves. If this process continues, there will simply be no hope for preventing a Chinese-dominated future for the world. Having come from North Korea, it is difficult to convey how depressing this all is. The horror of North Korea is Exhibit A of what a more Chinese world would look like: more unspeakable crime, more abject human suffering, more terrifying exploitation of innocent people for the benefit of a communist party cadre. Instead of ending the North Korean nightmare, Chinese hegemony promises only to spread the North Korean experience to more people around the world.

11

Real Tyranny and Real Freedom

"Even when you think you're alone, the birds and mice can hear you whisper." That was the first lesson I remember my mother teaching me as a child growing up in North Korea. Whether she meant it literally or believed it sincerely was irrelevant, because as a mother seeking to protect the physical safety of her children, it was the right lesson to teach us. That is the vicious cycle of speech and thought control that tyrannical governments deploy—even if you believe it's nonsense that the Dear Leader can "read your mind," you know it's not nonsense at all that his cronies can have you executed if you do or say anything wrong. So you might as well *act* like he *can* read your mind. Because in physical reality, the result is the same. The North Korean regime has annihilated any form of internal opposition through this type of censorship, fear, intimidation, and "reeducation."

A big challenge for defectors is that even when we make it to freedom, like I have in America, we often lack the vocabulary to describe what life in North Korea was like. When the only word you have ever been taught or permitted to use to describe your environment is *paradise*, it's not clear to you that it's actually "hell"—even if your animal instincts tell you that something is very, very wrong. Likewise, if you don't know that real freedom exists, then you will never know that real slavery exists, too, and thus you'll never understand that you, in fact, are one of its victims—a slave in your own country. When I was a child, I thought "freedom" (insofar as I had at my disposal any available words or concepts to grasp such an idea) meant independence from American Bastards and Japanese imperialists. When I got a little older, and started to plan my escape from North Korea, I thought it meant a bowl of rice, a full stomach. When I got a little older still, and was planning my escape from China, I thought it meant wearing blue jeans and watching television. When I came to America, I thought it meant learning.

Now, at age twenty-nine, having spent the last eight years in my new home, my English improving every day, I feel I've finally come to the point where I can describe in words what freedom and slavery are, and what it means to live in North Korea—approximately. Through books, videos, and speeches, I'm trying to paint an accurate portrait of what it's like to be a slave in that country. I believe it's important to do so—as an escaped slave, as a free woman, as an American, it is my right and duty to recover the language I never had to describe the bondage of my youth, and that of the poor souls still enslaved there.

North Korea is a socialist state, a surviving vestige of the Marxist-Leninist dream of a communist culmination of human history: a nuclear-armed, totalitarian dictatorship that has enslaved 26 million human beings into a cult of personality around three evil men, two of them dead, who have overseen a country-sized concentration camp.

The abject nightmare that has repeated itself every minute, every second, for seventy-four years within its borders is not the result of natural disaster, like in Haiti or Bangladesh, or colonialist imperialism, like in the Belgian Congo, or ethnic and religious factionalism, as in Syria or Iraq. It is the Earth's longest-running experiment in *deliberately managed* human misery, a perpetual crime against God, an interminable violation of human dignity, a black mark on the human species so dark and deep that it can almost make you ashamed to be a part of it—that it can make the individual human beings incarcerated there spend the entirety of their short lives dreaming and daydreaming of living instead as a bird, or even a mouse.

The horror of North Korea is evidenced in our very bodies. The availability of food and basic nutrients to North Koreans, including children and babies, has been so limited so frequently that it has split the genetically identical Korean ethnic people into different *physical* categories, with the Koreans under communism living shorter lives than their capitalist brethren, growing to shorter heights and reaching lower weights, with all the attendant consequences for rates of organ failure, susceptibility to disease, and cognitive development. All the generosity and kindness and altruism in the world can do nothing to reverse the damage: Of all the international food aid sent to North Korea, only a small percentage makes it into the hands and mouths of people who are malnourished, food insecure, or starving to death. The vast majority of the aid is intercepted, held, and meagerly rationed by the elite in Pyongyang, who have boasted in public of having achieved the impressive feat of keeping 10 percent of the population fed during times of famine.

There is a reason North Korea is known as the "hermit kingdom." There is no internet, no radio or television that isn't controlled directly and comprehensively by the government. All news broadcasts and other programming in North Korea are designed to trap the viewing population into a continuous, never-ending cycle of propaganda and brainwashing. Many defectors find themselves in a genuine state of shock when they realize, for the very first time, that Americans do not in fact have horns, or cold, scaly, reptilian skin, the way they do in every North Korean depiction. Defectors likewise find themselves in awe of the sheer number of cars that have packed the streets of America and South Korea for several decades. Perhaps the biggest surprise of all is when defectors first learn, and finally learn to accept, that there was no nuclear explosion at the end of the Korean War, and that North Korea did not "win" the war—that these are both lies. The only analogy I can even think of to better describe the experience of a North Korean defector is taking the red pill in *The Matrix*.

Even if you keep quiet in North Korea—even if you stay silent, keep to yourself, and accept your fate, including the fact that you don't have enough food to eat—there is still not a single civil liberty to which you are entitled. The threshold for being sent to a camp is almost comically low. If the authorities see that dust has gathered in the corners of a frame of a portrait of the Dear Leader—if a child is caught whistling a made-up tune that isn't a government-approved song—three generations of a family can be rounded up, imprisoned, and shot, "to wipe out the seed of dissent." The first rule of winding up in a North Korean concentration camp is to never, ever ask why you're there. It can lengthen your sentence, or lead directly to execution, or to the arrest and imprisonment of your family or friends. In 1997, the top-ranking official Hwang Jang-yop defected from North Korea. Hwang was the man who, incidentally, came up with the ideology of *Juche*, and the *Washington Post* later described his escape "as if Joseph

Goebbels had defected from Nazi Germany." Shortly thereafter, his wife died by "suicide," his daughter died by "falling off a truck," and the rest of his family—many of whom didn't even know they were related to him—were sent to concentration camps. Now, when high-level officials travel abroad to China, for example, their families are held hostage in camps until they return.

Many of the eleven thousand defectors from North to South Korea have provided testimony in recent years about the network of camps that spans the country. Matching their accounts to aerial footage and photographs taken by drones, stealth planes, and satellites, South Korean, Japanese, and Western intelligence have developed a fairly sophisticated understanding of which camps serve which purposes: imprisonment, hard labor, torture, execution, and the like. The largest and most famous of the camps, which has sometimes been compared with the horrors of Auschwitz, was Yodok, which is said to have been repurposed in 2014 but at its height held tens and maybe hundreds of thousands of inmates. Yodok was separated into a "revolution-ary zone," a reeducation camp used to punish people for crimes like speaking about government policy and illegally listening to foreign broadcasts, and a "total control zone," a prison camp for people con-sidered "enemies of the regime." Inmates who entered the total con-trol zone never left.

Outside the camps, cruelty is on display almost everywhere you look. Public executions remain a normal occurrence in North Korean cities and villages. Before hangings take place, the regime goons carrying them out will often fill the victim's mouth with rocks and secure it shut so they cannot speak any final words of dissent. Some-times victims have to be dragged to the hanging site because their bones have been broken and joints dislocated from hours of torture.

Almost invariably, before the person is hanged, the authorities bring the accuser's family out first to publicly denounce and stone them, so that the last thing they see before they die is the people they love most in the world being made to participate in their murder. A different form of execution is known as "hot boxing," in which a naked human being is locked inside a metal box for weeks without food or water, and sweats to death.

When female defectors to China are discovered and returned to North Korea, they often arrive pregnant with a Chinese man's child. In these cases, the regime will typically do whatever is necessary to force the woman to abort the fetus. Sometimes this will involve injecting the pregnant woman (or girl, as is often the case) with a syringe filled with some unsanitized solution, which infects and kills the fetus (and sometimes the mother). In other cases it simply involves jackbooted police or other regime authorities kicking the pregnant woman's stomach until she vomits, or placing a wooden board on her belly and forcing children to jump on it to crush the fetus. If somehow, through all this, a baby is still born, they will sometimes put the newborn child in a box to die. Such is the "racial purity" of North Korea preserved.

The North Korean regime has long been in possession of not just nuclear weapons, but chemical and biological weapons, too. So-called criminals from among the population are sometimes chosen to participate in "studies" or "experiments" from which they never emerge, dying from poison gases or weaponized infectious agents. Scientists, engineers, and other specialists supplied by the Chinese and Russian regimes have been pivotal to the Kim dynasty's ability to maintain such programs.

These weapons of mass destruction not only wreak havoc on

North Korean civilians, but serve as an effective deterrent to the out-side world. That deterrent is supplemented by the country's military, the fourth-largest active force in the world (following China, India, and the United States), with 1.28 million soldiers, as well as the second-largest military by total size after Vietnam's, estimated at 7.8 million people (including reservists and paramilitary forces). This means that one out of every three human beings in North Korea is somehow en-gaged in the "Korean People's Army," a gruesome institution reminis-cent of medieval slave armies. Conscription consists of an astonishing ten years of mandatory service for all North Korean men and at least seven years for women. The living and quality-of-life conditions for people in the army are unsurprisingly horrific, and women are some-times worked so hard that their bodies' menstrual cycles break down and they stop having periods. Sexual assault of female soldiers is, of course, endemic.

Even after North Koreans complete their mandatory military ser-vice, they don't have it much better as civilians. Periodic "collective mobilizations" consist essentially of hard labor, with wake-up calls at 5 a.m. and returning home around 8 p.m. The work itself is back-breaking, mostly digging in coal mines or iron refineries in rural areas. It often involves children as young as ten years old, and there is no retirement age beyond which one is no longer obligated to take part. "We are all revolutionaries," it is said—in other words, it is a privilege to die for the regime.

I spell out the utter brutality of physical life in North Korea in de-tail here because it is the only way I can convey the fact that it is noth-ing compared with the psychological damage. When I tell people this, they often have a hard time believing me—how could propaganda on TV or agitprop in classrooms actually be worse than literal imprisonment, torture, or execution? But it is. In most places in North Korea, there are weekly mutual criticism sessions, in which every citizen is assigned to a small cohort of other citizens, and they all gather to report and inform on each other, confess each other's shortcomings, accuse each other of wrongdoings, and punish each other through shame and social ridicule. In cities like my hometown of Hyesan, these meetings could be extremely intense; in rural areas like Kowon, where my mother was born, they were brutal. The people in this very isolated and patriotic part of the country genuinely thought of themselves as revolutionaries. There was no underground movement, no freedom fighters, no *résistance*. With no exposure to the world beyond the borders of their country or even their province, their devotion to the regime never waned; they never compromised in their fervor.

All regimes are capable of violence and abuse. But more than torture or imprisonment or corporal punishment, it is the *mental* enslavement of Kowon that remains for me the embodiment of socialism.

THE CIRCUMSTANCES that lead to the creation of a country like North Korea are in some ways unique and extraordinary. The Korean peninsula first had to be annexed by Imperial Japan, which was then caught in its own vicious authoritarian spiral, seeking to outcompete the empires of Europe for territory and geopolitical power in Asia. After the chaos and destruction of two world wars, the Japanese surrender, and the dissolution of the Japanese Empire, Korea had to be divided into two different zones, the north occupied by the victorious Red Army, the south occupied by the victorious United States. Negotiations for reunification had to fail, and two separate governments had to form: the communists in the north, the capitalists in the south. Then there had to be a civil war, the Korean War of 1950, a bloody, murderous catastrophe triggered by an invasion by the north, which lasted three years and incurred the decisive participation of foreigners, China and the United States. And finally, there had to be not an end to the war or a peace treaty, but simply a ceasefire, with no formal peace ever having been negotiated, right up through the present day. It was only then, through this complicated series of historical events, that Kim Il Sung was able to consolidate his power over a ruined country, founding the dictatorship we know today.

Given all that, it seems not just unlikely, but *impossible* for a normal liberal democracy to ever become an autocracy, for a free market society to ever become a communist dictatorship, for a country that is neither occupied nor partitioned nor at war to fall into chaos like Korea did. But that isn't necessarily true. The type of breakdown in trust, social order, and services that can lead to political anarchy don't always require civil or world wars or imperialist conquest. It can happen even in peacetime, simply by the slow erosion of institutions and mores. The revolutions in France and Russia did not by themselves lead to dictatorships. For Napoleon and Stalin to become possible in the first place, the old regimes—of Louis XVI in France, of Nicholas II in Russia—first had to lose control of their countries through many years of political and societal decay, all of which occurred during peacetime, and in eras when no one thought the dissolution of the monarchies would ever be possible.

It is impossible not to notice that something similar is taking place in America today. The bipartisan consensus that steered the United States through the Cold War is gone. Today, there is very little countrywide consensus on any political or cultural matters. What's more, the internet, social media, and the twenty-four-hour news cycle have exposed the corruption and incompetence of many of our political and cultural elites, to the point where most Americans no longer have any faith or trust in their elites. This in turn has led to historically low levels of voter participation in local and state politics, declining rates of church attendance and religious belief, and plummeting rates of family formation. Unwilling to take responsibility for any of these categories of national decline, American elites have resorted to insisting that all this is somehow the fault or responsibility of a particular political faction (almost always "conservatives" or "Republicans," by which they simply mean "working-class" or "rural" or "white"), and that we must start banning certain books, censoring certain forms of speech, and kicking these "political enemies" off various free speech platforms.

Meanwhile, these same American elites have been selling off their own country to China, spending decades shipping as many American jobs to China as possible, eroding America's industrial and manufacturing base and supply chains, leaving the country vulnerable to external shocks like the pandemic and the war in Ukraine. Millions of ordinary Americans have been plunged into chaos and ruin in the process. The response from elites has not been to help these people, but to stigmatize them all as racists, bigots, transphobes, and insurrectionists, in order to justify their declining fortunes.

The United States still has some of the most robust constitutional protections of any country in the world, and the American people's basic decency, commitment to freedom and liberty, and skepticism of government will likely see us through. But the environment has become riper than one would hope for a true demagogue to exploit America's decrepit institutions, corrupt elites, and increasingly hopeless lower classes. We survived the Great Depression, two world wars,

9/11, the 2008 financial crisis, and the COVID-19 pandemic—but I worry about what will happen the next time a big surprise arrives on our shores. Will we have the cohesion, the belief in the rule of law, and the confidence in democracy to see us through? Or will we resort to trammeling the Bill of Rights, seeking to silence dissenters, muzzle freedom of speech, get rid of political enemies, and assent to the government assuming indefinite "emergency powers"?

Already, there are some Americans who are calling for this. Self-described socialists, or woke activists, or social justice warriors, or whatever they're called on any particular day, want to kick their ideological opponents off social media. They want to ban parents from having any say in what public schools teach their own children. They want to tell you what you can and can't put into your own body, and they want the right to cut their perceived enemies off from financial services. They want education in basic subjects like math and science to reflect certain political preferences, rather than physical reality. Meanwhile, they want their own children to be able to buy their way into elite institutions, without having to take or perform well on standardized tests—a "socialist paradise" for thee, but not for me. This is exactly why the most basic social services don't work in any socialist country.

In North Korea, medical care is so poor for exactly this reason: Students bribe their way into universities, where they are taught only the correct "political," "socialist" understanding of medicine. I still carry the scar of socialism on my right lower quadrant: When I was a child, I was misdiagnosed with appendicitis when I most likely had viral enteritis, which I was later told would have been easy to diagnose for any half-trained medical doctor. I carry it all over my body, in fact, due to the many years of malnutrition and living so close to the brink of starvation—a scar that has impacted everything from my ability to reach a healthy weight to the heightened risks of pregnancy and childbirth.

The reason I wrote this book is because for so long, I never had the language to describe either tyranny or freedom. Now that I'm finally starting to, I need you—the reader—to help me bring attention to the fact that millions of North Koreans are still being robbed of even the words to describe their horrible nightmare, and that America itself is not as safe from a similar fate as it might think.

12

Freedom Matters

Given the life I had in North Korea and China, people often ask me why I didn't take the opportunity in America to at last live a private life. Why did I choose to write books, make videos, and put myself out into the public eye in such a visible way—one that robs me of any real claim I might have had to peace and quiet?

The truth is that, when you write down your thoughts or speak your mind and decide to share it with the world for the first time, you never do it with the intention of someday becoming a public figure. Something like that only happens step-by-step, and the gravity of the decision only becomes clear later. When I first agreed to go on *Now On My Way to Meet You*, the TV show in South Korea, I didn't do it because I wanted to be some sort of star: I did it because the producers told me that it was probably the best chance I would ever have of reconnecting with my sister.

It was only after having been on the show for some period of time that I realized how little even South Koreans knew about North Korea. It wasn't that they didn't care or were willfully ignorant: They genuinely didn't know the depths of the horror taking place across their northern border, and when I spoke about it, many people expressed genuine sympathy and concern. By the time I was invited to the One Young World conference, I accepted because I figured that the more people I could educate about North Korea, the better chance we'd have of making a difference for the people still suffering there. When the video of my speech went viral, it convinced me to accept the offer of an opportunity to write a memoir. The idea behind the YouTube channel was based on the same reasoning. And so it went, step-by-step, until somewhat quickly I found myself being harassed by the Kim regime. My family members back in North Korea were forced to denounce me on television, and I was increasingly subjected to various attempts at harassment, censorship, threats of violence, slander, and scams even right here in America.

People often suspect that I must regret these decisions, and that I should have opted for a life of comfortable anonymity here on the great big American continent. There are certainly times when that sounds nice, but another truth is that I feel I'm living on borrowed time. I'm twenty-nine, but when I look at myself in the mirror and think back on my life so far, I feel that I must be closer to a thousand. These twenty-nine years have been packed with so much life and tumult, so much love and loss, and so many near misses and close brushes with death, that everything from here on out I consider to be a bonus. There's a certain sadness in that, perhaps, but it's also liberating. My father died never having spent a single moment of his life knowing what it felt like to be free. That was supposed to be my fate, too. But what he died never having tasted, I've been gorging on now for several years. I'm satiated. That's why I live now only for my son, for love, and for the promotion of human rights.

This is not how most North Korean defectors end up feeling, even many years after their escape. Until very recently, my older sister still struggled to make sense of what happened to us, and had become quite bitter. Unlike me, she didn't want anyone to know that she'd been trafficked when she was just sixteen. She wanted to act like she'd had a normal life, and had no problem integrating into a conservative, traditional society like South Korea's. But inside, she was struggling, and angry. There was even a prolonged period of time when she'd changed her name and blocked me; we didn't speak for two years. I'm very glad to say that in the spring of 2022, however, Eunmi finally decided to begin speaking out about her experience in North Korea and China, and she is learning English so that she can share it more widely. I'm very proud to be her little sister.

Personality differences of course account for the bulk of why defectors display such variation in their approaches to their own pasts. But I think there is an important moral element, too. Speaking out about our past is important for the people still imprisoned in North Korea and those still enslaved in China. We cannot make it to freedom ourselves only to pull up the drawbridge and regard everyone we left behind as on their own. We owe it to them to tell the world what they're going through.

All that said, there's also a certain element of randomness in how I've lived my life. And when I look back, I sometimes have the feeling that it was someone else who lived it—that it couldn't have been me. When I disobeyed my father's wish that I should never attempt to escape to South Korea—because the punishment for getting caught, he felt, was worse than sticking it out in North Korea—I think to myself:

Who was it that disobeyed her father like that? That had such courage? It couldn't have been me, certainly. So who was it?

Well, it was literally me, of course—but the older I get, the more
I realize it wasn't me alone. It was me, plus the fortitude given to
me by my parents, plus a whole lot of luck, plus a higher power I
don't pretend to understand. And that combination of strengths and
fortune still follows me wherever I go. The truth is, I don't actually
like giving speeches very much, or going to conferences or to social
events. I prefer to be at home with my son, or alone with books. But
it's always the memory of my parents and some larger force in the
universe that keeps urging me forward, constantly pushing me to do
more, write more, speak out more. I could take credit for all that, but
I'm old enough now to know that no one acts alone.

This is also why my encounter with therapy was relatively brief,
and I currently feel no need to return to it. I have no doubt that some
amount of therapy can be extraordinarily useful for certain people.
But for me, it couldn't take the place of meaning itself. When I found
meaning in my life—in being a mother, and in advocating for human
rights—I also found that it didn't matter what kinds of nightmares I
had, or how often I had them. No matter how much trouble I have
sleeping, or how awful my dreams, I always have a reason to get out
of bed in the morning, to be joyful, and most of all, to be grateful. My
American friends and colleagues often speak of the importance of "taking care of yourself" and "putting yourself first," and I don't necessarily
disagree. But it's not enough to "do you"—it's just as important, if not
more so, to have purpose, to set an example for your children, and to
devote yourself to something bigger. No amount of therapy, dieting,
meditation, or "self-care" can do what *meaning* can do.

I don't think it's possible to love America more than I do. But I would be lying if I didn't acknowledge that life in contemporary America can often make it hard to find that meaning. After being here for only a few years, I noticed it in my own life: The sheer abundance of material comfort had made me a bit soft and irritable in ways I never was before; the emphasis on individuality, "finding your own voice," and "living your own truth" made me a little less instinctively compassionate for other people than I had been; and I'd gotten into the habit of complaining when things didn't work, or when people made mistakes, or when events didn't go my way.

I remember being almost shocked at myself when I stayed at a hotel one night before a conference and the mattress was, objectively, very uncomfortable. I knew that when I woke up in the morning my back would hurt, and I got upset, knowing I'd paid a considerable amount of money just to have a bad night's sleep. I even felt a little self-righteous: I'd learned from many of my peers at Columbia that a certain level of cynicism and a certain amount of complaining is actually a sign of a discerning, sophisticated intelligence. So I decided to go down to the front desk to complain.

While I was waiting for the elevator, I saw my reflection in a mirror on the wall and immediately felt ashamed. Here I was, in a hotel, for God's sake, in the United States of America. It had a roof and a bed and food. And who was I? I was a girl with nothing but a hope and a dream, living on borrowed time. In this building I was safe and satiated and left alone to do and think as I please. What more did I need to make my dreams come true? A softer mattress?

It's a wonderful thing that so many people in America—including newcomers like me—have so many of their basic needs met that they're able to turn their attention to things like the plushness of hotel beds. But there's a danger in it, too. There are few people left in America who have ever faced starvation, or wondered where their next meal would come from. And as the generation of the Great Depression and the world wars passes on, so does the memory of what it took to build the system of abundance that we enjoy today. As America becomes predominantly made up of people who didn't have a hand in building the system in the first place, it is producing more and more people who want to destroy the system because they don't understand it. They don't appreciate how fragile their freedom is, how precious their system of government, how rare their way of life. And so they entertain fantasies of tearing it down. In some cases, those fantasies are becoming reality.

AMERICA IS a racist, imperialist, evil, greedy country that is more responsible than any other for war, injustice, cruelty, inequality, and terror around the world. We will never rest until American capitalism is overturned, the American military and police state are dissolved, and American democracy is exposed as nothing more than a corrupt sham."

Question: If you had to bet, to whom would you attribute this quote? A North Korean television broadcaster? An Iranian government cleric? A professor at Columbia? A U.S. congressperson?

My guess is you'd probably wager as little money as possible on such a bet, because it's genuinely too hard to know! It could just as easily be an ISIS general as a junior product manager at Twitter. To someone who's lived 50 percent of her life in each world—half in the anti-American authoritarian dictatorship, and half in the land of the free itself—this has been quite the shock. How did we get to the point where American children and North Korean children are being fed fairly similar propaganda about the United States?

The parallels are doubly shocking when you consider the kinds of people who espouse these views. In North Korea, the people you hear railing against America are underfed teachers, malnourished children, frightened parents, and elites whose livelihoods depend on the Kim crime family. That doesn't make their hatred and ignorance excusable, but at least it makes some sense. In America, however, the people railing against their own country are often overfed, or obsessed with intentionally limiting the amount of food they eat. Often they will "speak out" against American history, society, capitalism, and democracy on an American social-media platform from their American phone or computer, or on the campus of a world-class American university, or on the street with the permission of American government authorities and the protection of American police officers. North Koreans say such things because if they don't, they'll be shot. Americans do it because they think it's fun, or because they want to acquire power and influence over other people.

It's no wonder, really, that while millions of people around the world continue to face murder, starvation, rape, torture, and enslavement, many Americans who support "social justice" are primarily concerned with the infinite multiplication of ungrammatical gender pronouns and how much "range" to give chickens before they wind up in supermarkets. It's easy to laugh at this kind of childish, nonsensical behavior—even I enjoy poking fun at it now and again—but at the end of the day, unfortunately, it's deadly serious. When a people become untethered from history, when they become unshackled from reality, when they lose the ability to understand cause and effect, they become ripe for exploitation from those who hold real power.

Revolutions are typically thought of as violent, turbulent events—societal earthquakes that flood the streets and quickly alter (in most cases, destroy) the prevailing physical reality. The years 1776, 1789, 1848, and 1917 often come to mind. But there is a different kind of revolution, one that unfolds more modestly, almost imperceptibly. The new ideology might start in only a small number of classrooms, or magazines, or bureaucracies. You might notice it spreading, but comfort yourself that it's prevalent only among people below a certain age, and so they'll grow out of it; or popular only among people who work in certain industries or certain parts of the country. You tell yourself that those people all live in a "bubble," and that it's never long before bubbles pop. You're confident it's just a fad, and that it's never long before fads fade away, giving way to new fads.

But these little fringe ideas held by a small number of young people and immature adults in isolated industries located in eccentric parts of the country can slowly but surely become the entire society's dominant culture. Especially if the new ideology works to the advantage of political, financial, and cultural elites, they will be happy to adopt it as dogma in all the country's institutions of power. Some version of that process is what happened in Russia, China, and North Korea. There is a version of it happening now in America.

I don't say that to be needlessly provocative or melodramatic. Of course I don't think that America in 2023 is anything like Russia in 1917, or China in 1927, or North Korea in 1945. I say it only because if there is one thing I've learned in my life, it's that freedom and civilization are extraordinarily delicate. Travel around the world, and you will notice how indecent life is for most people in most countries. In many cases, it's not because a particular country has *never* built a functioning society before, it's because whatever free, tolerant, and relatively prosperous society they did build in the past was destroyed at some point in a fit of madness. Ronald Reagan said it best: "Freedom is a fragile thing and it's never more than one generation away from extinction. It is not ours by way of inheritance, it must be fought for and defended constantly by each generation, for it comes only once to a people. And those in world history who have known freedom and then lost it have never known it again."

What is this freedom that we need to preserve? Dear reader, it's right there in the Bill of Rights: freedom of religion, speech, press, assembly, and petition; the right to bear arms; freedom from unreasonable searches and seizures; the right to due process of law, freedom from self-incrimination, and the rights of accused persons; freedom from cruel and unusual punishments; the freedom of cities and states to make laws for themselves independently of the federal government.

We as Americans must fight to preserve these freedoms, because they are never more than a generation away from disappearing. This doesn't mean we have to harden our hearts, or lose our humanity or compassion. One thing I love so much about Americans is that—unlike any other people on the planet—when they face daunting challenges, they become *more* cheerful and hopeful, not less. As we brace ourselves for the fight of a lifetime, we mustn't forget who we are.

BUT WHAT can we, as individuals and as communities, actually do about all this?

We often think of July 4, 1776, as being America's one and only "founding." But the truth is that America has had multiple foundings, or re-foundings, throughout its history. The first founding was the establishment of colonies by religious refugees from England in the early seventeenth century, who saw themselves as building a New Jerusalem in the New World, practicing self-government under the light of God thousands of miles away from the religious persecution and violence of the Old World. But over the course of more than a hundred years, the relationship between the colonies and the British Crown became untenable. The long tentacles of imperial monarchy stretched across the Atlantic, robbing the American colonists of equal status in the British Empire, and stealing from them the opportunity to determine their own fate.

Thus a second founding was required: the Declaration of Independence from the British king, the Revolutionary War to win that independence by force of arms, and the passage of the Constitution. But even though the ratification of the Constitution led to the greatest and most profound system of democratic government ever established, the rights and freedoms it offered were extended to only a fraction of the population: first only to landowning aristocrats, and then, after the extension of the franchise, only to white male citizens. The creation of new states and their absorption into the Union as non-slave states disrupted the balance of power in the federal government, leading to secessionist passions in the slave-owning southern states and threatening the breakup of the Union.

And so a third founding became necessary. The victory of the Union over the Confederacy in the Civil War was not merely the victory of Northerners over Southerners or even just of abolitionists over slave owners: It was the victory of the idea of a *United* States over the attempt to break up the country into multiple separate warring states, like in Europe. The Union's victory re-founded America as a united country free of slavery and free of civil war. But the era of Reconstruction was tumultuous: Although slavery was abolished, the Jim Crow South still treated Black Americans as second-class citizens, and threatened them with unceasing violence. Meanwhile, the industrial economies of the North were leading to an era of untold inequality, reproducing Old World conditions of subjugated workers and indentured servants working for very little pay in harsh, dangerous conditions under the thumb of a wealthy oligarchy.

A fourth founding was born: the era of the New Deal and the Civil Rights Movement. The heroism of labor organizers fighting for working-class rights and civil rights leaders fighting for equal treatment for all races under the Constitution led to the country and society that Americans have enjoyed ever since. But again, as so often throughout our past, the social contract held together by this most recent founding has started to break down. The transition from an industrial to a digital and services economy has left many American workers without the opportunities they enjoyed after the establishment of the fourth founding; the decisions by many capital-owning Americans to ship U.S. jobs to China and elsewhere abroad have left many American workers angry and hopeless. What's more, the racial tensions that subsided after the victories of the Civil Rights Movement in the 1960s have reemerged. And immigration on a scale not seen since the beginning of the twentieth century—both legal and illegal—has flooded into the United States from Asia and Latin America, putting added stress on America's ailing system of social services. The relative social harmony of the 1980s and 90s has frayed. Americans have grown to distrust not only their institutions and political and business leaders, but each other.

Clearly, we are in for a fifth founding. This is no laughing matter. Many of our previous foundings have involved wars and civil conflict, stretching our system of government to the breaking point. Often, we made it through only because of the wisdom, foresight, and perseverance of a few mighty leaders—a species of American that is hard to find in Washington these days. There is no Washington, no Jefferson, no Lincoln or Roosevelt or King to guide the leaky ship of American self-government through the rocky waters of the twenty-first century.

For this reason, I believe our fifth founding will involve the re-establishment of personal responsibility and local government. For too long, we have looked to our national government in Washington, D.C., to solve all our problems and to resolve all of our differences. But it is not the job of the president to fix your local school system; it is not the job of the Supreme Court to make decisions for your family or community. It is *your* job—and mine, and all of ours—to partici-pate every day in self-government, not just to outsource democratic government to politicians.

So go to your city council hearings. Attend your local school board meetings. Get involved in your homeowners association. Join civic groups that convene people with common interests. Raise money to bring artists and performers from around the country to your town. Become a leader in your local house of worship, and give back to the poor and the needy. Coach your children's sports teams. Talk to them about America and our shared history together at the dinner table. Read books to them at night. Make sure they give back to their com-munities. Limit your exposure to social media. Constrain your diet of talk radio and cable news. Ignore most of what happens in Washing-ton. Become the master of your domain.

Spend a month, or even just a week, forgetting about what hap-pens in Washington and concentrating on the happiness and im-provement of your own family and community, and I promise you will suddenly feel differently about America. You will feel more hopeful, more optimistic, more compassionate, more disciplined, and more determined to improve the future than ever before. The light of your example will shine so brightly that no woke mob will be able to extinguish it—in fact they will be embarrassed by it, because deep down, they know that they have nothing whatsoever to offer free, prosperous, patriotic individuals and communities. Don't be cowed by them. Don't give up on our country.

My father is the one who taught me to never, ever give up. Even on his deathbed, he encouraged me to keep pressing forward and to find a way to overcome challenges. This was a man who'd spent his life in a nightmare, in and out of prisons, often starving and beaten, who spent his final days ridden with cancer. This was the man who told his young daughter to never give in, never surrender—because life itself is precious.

If my father felt that way about the life he lived in North Korea and China, what would he have thought had he lived to see America? I'm certain he would have thought it was nothing less than a miracle. Just as I do.

Warriors of the Light

Sometime in 2019, I'd started to sense a rift in my marriage. The bonds that had brought us so close together when we first married had begun to perceptibly loosen until we both felt that the fraying had become irreversible. Later in 2020, we separated and eventually divorced. Although I knew it was ultimately for the best, I still couldn't shake the reality that in the one thing I'd grown to care most about in life—my own family—I'd failed. Was there something wrong with me?

Divorce is always tricky, of course, and ours carried the acute complication of sharing our lovely son. As parents to this wonderful child who remained so devoted to him, we decided that the best decision for him was to all stay in the same city, to both stay equally involved in his life and upbringing, and that we would do everything in our power to continue to instill the right values in him, which my ex-husband and I continued to share.

Because my young son is at the very center of my life, I think a lot these days about which values I want to instill in him, and what kinds of human beings I should hold up to him as role models. This has been more difficult and less intuitive for me than it might be for other American mothers. After spending the first half of my life in North Korea and China, I was convinced that no one in the world was good except for the people in my own family—that everyone else was in some way a liar, or a manipulator, or a force for evil. This is the inevitable consequence of being taught, from the time you are a child, that enemy spies and evil forces are everywhere, including among your neighbors and in your own home. Growing up, I was never in the habit of thinking of other human beings as being "role models," or as setting good examples for others, or as embodying certain values. There were just my parents and sister, who were good; every other human being on earth, who was bad; and the Dear Leader, who was God.

I have since been disabused of this notion after spending time in South Korea and especially in America, but it has still been a struggle to approach people with the trust that might come easily to others. Yet my encounters with some remarkable souls in North America have convinced me to look at things differently. I realize now that there is a light in everyone, and that almost all people really are truly good at heart—some just have a harder time accessing that light than others.

I'm very fond of a lesson taught by Jordan Peterson, which he calls "Choose Your Own Sacrifice." The idea is that, in every individual human being's path of development, we go from children with limitless possibilities to adults who must decide on what, specifically, to focus and to what to dedicate the rest of our lives. This process of homing in on a specific mission or goal or life project requires us to forsake all the other possibilities that were open to us when we were children, and this is often a painful and difficult process. That's why choosing your life's work is, ultimately, a process of sacrifice, of forsaking. We sacrifice our "pluripotentiality," to use the technical jargon, in order to become mission-oriented and develop skills that are world-class in one particular area. While choosing your own sacrifice is hard, and in some ways sad, it is also what allows us to eventually generate the greatest amount of value for our families and our communities. And using your own talents and achievements to benefit others is one of the hallmarks of living a good, responsible, and rewarding life.

For me, of all the different ways that I could choose to spend my life, the one I'm attempting to zero in on is the protection and promotion of human rights—specifically the right of individual freedom. Despite the deprivation of my early life, all the comforts and material gains in the world now mean nothing to me unless I can share and enjoy them with people who are now undergoing the same horrors I endured in my childhood.

This life project has brought me into contact with others who share a similar mission, and who see their purpose on this earth in much the same way. These people are modern-day freedom fighters, who stand up to the forces of authoritarianism they see in their communities and society, and see it as their calling to set a good example to others of a free life well lived. Paulo Coelho, one of my favorite authors, refers to such people as "warriors of the light." These are generally individuals who are smart, driven, and capable enough to be living lavish lives of success in the corporate world, but who decide instead to dedicate their lives to fighting for freedom. I want to close this book by thanking three who I see not only as personal role models but role models for my son.

AT THIS point you've probably gleaned my admiration for Dr. Jordan Peterson, former Harvard professor of clinical psychology, now professor emeritus at the University of Toronto, and the bestselling author of the seminal volumes *12 Rules for Life: An Antidote to Chaos* and its sequel, *Beyond Order: 12 More Rules for Life*. Dr. Peterson's books have been translated into forty-five languages, a testament to the connection he's been able to forge with his readers. His philosophy of personal responsibility and how to live a meaningful life has made him a personal hero of mine, and his books will remain on my shelf for as long as I live, a passion I hope to one day share with my son.

Through his daughter Mikhaila, I was able to meet Dr. Peterson and speak with him about my experience growing up in North Korea and the parallels with wokeism at Columbia. His experience and training as a clinical psychologist shone through: I'd never spoken to another human being before who demonstrated such a degree of authentic empathy and genuine understanding. Our interview over Zoom was the first time I ever felt safe and comfortable enough to vocally share the details of my past with someone who wasn't a family member or lifelong friend. After the interview, Dr. Peterson continued to stay in touch about how to spread my message more broadly, and my own audience expanded rapidly after my appearance on his show.

One thing we have in common is our mutual fascination with and deep disdain for tyrannical regimes. Dr. Peterson is a collector of original propaganda art from the Soviet era, and the walls of his home in Toronto are covered in it. Though politically non-aligned, he is one of the Western world's foremost authorities on Marxism and the history of socialist thought, which he continues to write about and debate with other leading intellectuals. (When he goes up against a self-professed Marxist, he always wins.)

As the years have gone on, and I've been subjected to more and more efforts at online harassment, "canceling," and the like, I've developed even more admiration for Dr. Peterson, who has been the woke movement's Public Enemy #1 since the beginning. It has never stopped him from continuing to be honest and forthright about his own views and principles. The reason he's become uncancelable and remains more popular than ever is because of that authenticity: You can't fool ordinary viewers, listeners, and readers into thinking you have opinions that you don't actually have. Genuineness is an appealing and admirable quality that puts you above partisan bickering, and makes the example you set more important to people than any particular opinion you might hold. Dr. Peterson is "realness" personified, and I keep him in mind whenever I communicate with an audience.

Perhaps the single thing that has made me such a fan of Dr. Peterson and his work is the way he's able to combine intellectual self-confidence with intellectual humility. "I act as if God exists," is one of my favorite lines of his. He doesn't dogmatically say that God does or doesn't exist, and he doesn't pretend that he has the ability to prove it one way or another. He simply believes that *if* God exists, it's probably a good thing, and even if He doesn't, people who conduct their lives as if He does will live more purposeful, rich, and rewarding lives. He doesn't make this point and others like it in order to sound smart, or to gain influence or power, or to secure book publishing deals and land cocktail party invitations. He does it because he is a person with bedrock convictions and wants to share them with as many people as possible—predominantly young people who are struggling to be happy and adjust to life in the modern world, as he did when he grew up. He doesn't sit in judgment of others, or try to proselytize others to his way of life: He simply serves as an example of how one might live a better life, and for that I am thankful.

HE'S BEEN in the public eye for three decades, but in the last few years, Joe Rogan has become a ubiquitous household name: a central figure in American culture and a barometer of changing cultural patterns. Hugely popular with a wide and demographically diverse audience, the *Joe Rogan Experience* has been the top podcast in the United States for some time. His appeal lies in being exceptionally thoughtful and curious while remaining unusually humble and open. He doesn't pretend to know about things he doesn't, which is why he invites others to come on the show and teach him (and his listeners). That formula sounds so intuitive and obvious that it should also be widespread, but it isn't. Most media figures see their job as delivering prepackaged opinions to what they think of as highly gullible viewers and listeners; Rogan has more respect for his audience than that. His values are curiosity, humor, heart, and common sense. And lo and behold, the market for that kind of content is world-beating.

I was thrilled but extremely nervous when I received an invitation to appear on *JRE* in Austin, Texas. I had seen interviews before where a guest tried to show off his or her intellect or accomplishments, and by simply asking a few straightforward, good-faith questions, Rogan (intentionally or not) exposed their posturing. I was warned repeatedly by friends that while Rogan is relaxed, friendly, and creates a welcoming environment, don't be deceived into thinking that you don't need to prepare: If you say something that doesn't make sense, or that sounds wrong, or that he knows the audience will have questions about, he won't hesitate to raise the issue.

Alas, my fears were unfounded. Rogan was a consummate gentleman before, during, and after the show. Our recorded conversation lasted over three hours, but it went by so fast that when it ended, I thought it had been less than an hour, and was worried he'd cut it short because I wasn't good. Unlike nearly every other interviewer I've come across in popular media, Rogan wasn't interested in "gotchas" or in creating a controversy or making his guest look stupid or inferior. He was simply interested in learning about the human rights catastrophe in North Korea and China's active role in propagating it, which he'd heard and read about but wanted to better understand. He also dug deeper into the details of the story of my escape from North Korea to China and then to South Korea than anyone I'd ever spoken with before, and I could tell that he was listening attentively, with both an active mind and an open heart. In particular, I remember marveling at how his questions—which were clearly well-informed and prepared—were developed with the utmost sincerity and casualness, as if we were just two old friends catching up. It's no wonder people who can only handle little sound bites from other media outlets are happy to listen to Rogan's podcasts for three to four hours at a time.

My favorite part of the interview was when we discussed my experience at Columbia, because Rogan came to the dangers of the woke movement earlier than most. His core insight was that the current generation is able to withstand so little adversity and reverts to shouting and crying so easily because they've never had to endure truly hard times, like all earlier generations have. "Hard times create strong men, strong men create good times, good times create weak men, and weak men create hard times" was the bit of wisdom he shared with me (from the novel *Those Who Remain*, by G. Michael Hopf).

Rogan's willingness to be open and honest has put him in the crosshairs of the government and activist pressure, but he has stood his ground, preserved his integrity, and maintained his commitment to free speech. The basic decency with which he conducts himself is something I think about a lot. It's not easy to be that kind or generous or compassionate. I don't assume it comes easily to anyone. It takes work to connect with your fellow human beings as deeply as Rogan does. It is an example toward which everyone should strive.

ANOTHER WONDERFUL individual I was fortunate to meet was Candace Owens. An outspoken African-American woman who is not afraid to stick her neck out by debunking critical race theory and extreme antiracism doctrines, Owens came to light as a force of nature after testifying to Congress in 2019 on "confronting white supremacy," using data to point out that very little if any of the explanation for crime (even racially motivated crimes) in America is reducible to the "tyranny of the white man." Her memoir, *Blackout*, is likewise a moving account of her early life and her later political awakening—it was a big influence on my decision to write an account of my own experience. In 2021, Candace joined *The Daily Wire*, cofounded by the conservative commentator and media host Ben Shapiro.

I had met Shapiro when he interviewed me on his show toward the end of 2020. I really enjoyed his take on many topics, especially his now-infamous line, "Facts do not care about your feelings." He also spoke intelligently on the concept of meritocracy and had Peterson-esque practical advice to listeners on how to live fulfilling and responsible lives by refusing to blame others for their own circumstances. Needless to say, I was pleasantly surprised when I received an invitation to visit *The Daily Wire* headquarters in Nashville for an interview with Candace.

I was not disappointed. *The Daily Wire* staff were exceptionally hospitable and professional. After an hour of answering interview questions with the social-media team, I was led to another studio where *The Candace Owens Show* is recorded. I met her briefly before the segment and gave her a signed copy of *In Order to Live* as a thank-you.

She was an extremely talented interviewer who asked penetrating questions about my life in North Korea, the story of my escape, and the difficulties I endured in China. We also touched on certain parallels that we both know exist in contemporary American society. At the end of the interview, Owens was surprised to see her audience rise for a standing ovation for the two of us. Apparently, that hadn't happened before in the show's history.

I remember sitting there, an immigrant from North Korea with a thick accent, next to Candace Owens, a young Black woman, and watching the diverse audience applaud and smile. This, I thought to myself, is America.

Acknowledgments

I don't know what I did to deserve all the love and support I've received in life, but I want to briefly acknowledge the immeasurable gratitude I feel every day to be surrounded by truly incredible human beings.

First, I want to thank Jeremy Stern for helping me bring this book to life and for the pleasure of our many conversations. I am also deeply grateful to my agent, Jonathan Bronitsky from ATHOS, and my magnificent editors, Natasha Simons and Mia Robertson from Simon & Schuster, for believing in me.

My partner in crime, Dr. Rouzbeh Ahmadian, was with me every step of the way in the process of writing this book, from helping craft the first draft until proofreading the final pages. He has been my rock through everything, and his humor never fails to put a smile on my face. I have also been so thankful to be welcomed into his family with open arms: Morteza, Faranak, Roshi, and Jerry—thank you.

Even though I lost much of my family in North Korea and China, many people have become my family since, among them the amazing staff members of the Human Rights Foundation. Thor Halvorssen has been the brother I never had, who's taught me everything from how to eat lobster to understanding the meaning of unconditional love and joy, in life and in relationships. I am also thankful for Alex Gladstein, Alex Lloyd and his lovely wife Rachel, Colby Thomson, Celine Boustani, Garry Kasparov, and Enes Kanter Freedom.

I still can't believe I've had the honor to become friends with some of my role models and heroes. I am grateful beyond words to Dr. Jordan B. Peterson, Mikhaila Peterson, Joe Rogan, Lex Fridman, Patrick Bet-David, Mario Aguilar, Tim Pool, Robert Kiyosaki, Dave Rubin, Bari Weiss, Candace Owens, Ben Shapiro, Melissa Chen, Faisal Saeed Al Mutar, Masih Alinejad, Dinesh D'Souza, Douglas Murray, Dennis Prager, and Marissa Streit from PragerU, and Tim Ballard, Hayden Paul, Vessie Pearson, and Jeremiah Evans, from Operation Underground Railroad.

Other friends and colleagues to whom I am indebted for their support and love include Karolina Sutton from Curtis Brown, Amanda Urban and Billy Hallock at ICM Partners, Maryanne Vollers, James Chau, Matthew Tyrmand, Drew Binsky, Austin Wright, Chris Chappell, Emma-Jo Morris from the *New York Post*, Grace Forest, Will Witt, Casey Lartigue Jr., Esther Paik Vess, Blaine Vess, Sarah Son, Daniele Carettoni, Genevieve Wolff Jurvetson, Steve Jurvetson, Matt Mullenweg, Jordan Harbinger, Hyram, and Leeann Roybal-Shin.

I also want to thank my supporters, especially John Mitchel, Dave Rice, and all those who have helped me across social media platforms.

I am thankful to my ex-husband for being a wonderful father to our son and to Dory, Eileen, and George.

I am grateful beyond words for my mother, who is my best friend. There are no words that can express how thankful I am for all the sacrifices she made for me and my sister, let alone for giving us the gift of life. Without her my son could never exist, and for that alone I am indebted to her for eternity.

Lastly, to my son: I still can't believe I am a mother to such a precious, loving, and kind person. You are the dream of your grandmother, your grandfather, and me. The dreams of our ancestors continue to live through you, and we will all be with you wherever you go in life. I am in awe, and I love you.